Joie de Vivre

Judith Northwood-Boorman

Illustrations by Judith Northwood-Boorman, unless otherwise stated.

Published by Feedaread.com

First Edition

A CIP catalogue record for this title is available from the British Library.

Other books by author:

Georgia's Fantastic Christmas (1996)

Dum. Mad or Just Plain Blonde? (2006)

Georgia's Fantastic Christmas & Other Stories (2013)

Acknowledgements

With thanks to all of those who have contributed in some way to this book, but special thanks to Susan Pope for her initial reading and corrections.

Also Sarah Martin for her proof-reading and inspiration. She was always the best story writer in our class and I only beat her once in English. That was in the first year when I came top.

Anne Humphrey and Anne Matthews for their HOGS contributions.

Marnie Summerfield-Smith's objective editorial eye helped a lot.

Greg Northwood for help with the cover.

Christine Hamilton for formatting assistance.

Exceptional mention of course to Ralph. He puts up with a lot.

There may still be a few slips and trips in the text.

Feel feel to let me know.

Contact me via Facebook 'Joie de Vivre'.

I dedicate this book to my sadly missed family, Dad (Jim Stow), Mum (Sylvia, aka Topsy Stow) and Sister (Gillian Aird).

'Life would be tragic if it weren't funny'

Stephen Hawking

INTRODUCTION

Joie de Vivre

'Joie de Vivre' seems to be the most appropriate title for this collection.

It was a great compliment when Linda Tidy (fellow editor of our Medway Mermaids' Anthology 'Mermaid Tales') suggested I was 'a very joyful person'. The fact I'd already started this anthology, her kind comment seemed an endorsement.

So why the title?

Well, I guess I am a bit of a Francophile. After spending seven years studying French, primarily with our scary French teacher, Miss Holl, the love of everything French evolved.

My love affair was then firmly established after the most wonderful month in France, as au pair, aged eighteen. 'The Joy of Flying Solo' is my account of setting out for that fantastic opportunity. It left a lasting impression on me. I did write a journal at the time, which I still have and maybe that will be another book.....

I only saw the Cayrols, my host family, one time subsequently. During my first term at university, I got a message from my landlady that my parents were trying urgently to get hold of me. Bernard and Dany were in London, and had called my home number from "Arrods'. They were staying in Kensington and asked if we could meet up that evening. So I jumped straight on a train home, where we then went up to Kensington to meet my lovely French friends in a restaurant. Needless to say my dad insisted on paying the bill, as they had looked after me so well during my stay.

In May 2013, I was finally reunited with some of the Cayrols, when I revisited Le Cres. For over thirty years Mum had kept the communication going with the Cayrols, with a card at Christmas. I re-established contact after Mum died but was rather mystified by the absence of any mention of Bernard in Dany's cards or letters.

I suspected a vitriolic divorce (he was a bit of a charmer) but I didn't want to raise the subject myself. Maybe the mystery would be disclosed when we visited?

Ralph had decided on the French wine route tour after I had won a weekend in Bordeaux in 2013. It seemed a good opportunity to have an early holiday in May. After flying to Bordeaux, enjoying our two night freebie at the Ibis Style, we hired a car and made our way to Montpellier. It took us eight days, as we like to take the scenic routes.

It was a wonderful, wonderful trip.

We visited Saint-Émilion, on the way. By chance it happened to be their 'Portes Ouvertes' weekend where all the chateaux open their doors to the public and give free wine tastings. What a result. It is a truly beautiful town with some equally beautiful wines. Hic! We wished we were staying there but we had booked a B&B, La Muscadelle, at Monbazillac (a small village outside Bergerac). Our tour then took us to Siorac, St Cirque La Popie, Cordes sur Ciel (two stunningly beautiful medieval villages perched on hillsides) and Peyriac Minervois.

We made the mistake of not allowing enough time for our reunion. It was only half way through our tour that I received an e-mail from Dany announcing that Emmanuelle and her two daughters Eve and Leah were visiting from Paris. They however would be leaving after lunch on Sunday. We on the other hand, had not planned to arrive until Sunday afternoon. I really could not miss the opportunity to see my eight-year-old charge as a grown woman with children of her own. We made sure we left Peyriac Minervois early to arrive before Emmanuelle and her girls left. Sadly things never go quite according to plan. We were stuck in a 'bouchon' (traffic jam) for over an hour. An unfortunate motorist had lost his caravan. The wreckage of the flimsy shell of the mobile holiday home was strewn along the hard shoulder; pillows, duvets, pots, pans and clothes creating a show stopping spectacle.

But luckily we did arrive in time to see the whole family together. Emmanuelle speaks excellent English; she lived in London for three years and in fact Eve, now thirteen, was born in London. The thirty six years evaporated; I could still glimpse the eight year old in this forty four year old woman. Petite, pretty, with a beautiful curly mane of light brown hair with golden streaks. She also solved the mystery of her 'missing' father. He did leave her mum for a much younger, horse mad woman. He too became passionate about horse riding but was thrown from his horse. He suffered a severe head trauma and finally died after three years in a vegetative state. Not only did he leave a young widow but a young daughter, his older children, Emmanuelle and Claire also an ex-wife who couldn't bear to mention his name.

It was a very sad tale. No 'Joie de Vivre' in that story, I'm afraid.

In the evening, we took Dany for a meal in Montpellier. I knew that this reunion would severely test my French conversational skills. For months beforehand I had been revising my French, reading Penguin dual translation short stories and listening to BBC's French course on the way to work. I was hoping to improve Ralph's French too. I'd also had a few lunch time 'conversation classes' with my French speaking colleague from Cameroon. It paid off as I was able to keep the conversation going for the whole evening, translating for Ralph when he didn't catch the drift. I was even able to speak to Claire, the younger daughter, who rang her mum whilst we were in the restaurant. She is now a paediatrician living on a farm in Cannes, with her three horses, dogs, cats and chickens.

Now we have our very own French family.

Daughter-in-law Marie, despite her British passport is very French, having been born and educated in Paris. Sophie and James, our grandchildren, will at some point become bi-lingual.

It seems only right that the 'French Connection' is formally acknowledged. 'Joie de Vivre' seems a perfectly suitable title.

So please join me in celebrating my eclectic mixture of 'joys'. I apologise in advance if some seem ironic or at times, sad.

THE JOY OF TRAVEL

I would like to dedicate this section to Solange Hando, award winning travel writer, who has visited Medway Mermaids twice, sharing her sound advice and inspiration

THE JOY OF FLYING SOLO

August 1977

We'd finally heaved my bulging 'Taurus' suitcase into the boot of Dad's gleaming Sahara yellow Cavalier.

'Are you taking lead weights with you?' he jokes, then wrapping his arms around my shoulder pecks me on the cheek, adding, 'We're going to miss you, love. But I suppose we'd better get used to it, eh? I expect we'll only see you once a term when you're in Canterbury.'

That sharp pain of sadness prickles at my nose, as tears well in the corners of my eyes. I am willing them not to roll from my tired and overloaded eyelids. I don't have a Handy Andy handy. I'd packed them in my suitcase. Besides that, I'm a big girl now and big girls don't cry. At least that's what the irritating lyrics of that song tell us.

I slip onto the cool vinyl of the car seat but the tears trickle despite my best efforts. I sniffle, trying to keep the snot from dripping too. I succeed, breathing in at the same time, the slightly unpleasant aroma of plastic. Dad's pride and joy, this first brand new car, still has that showroom smell.

'Where's your Mum?' Dad asks, slightly exasperated.

'Probably checking I haven't forgotten anything. She's been poking about in my suitcase for the last three days, reminding me of this and that. Despite my list, I'm bound to have forgotten something.'

We watch Mum locking the door. She waves something at me...a blue and pink box. Oh no, how embarrassing.

Opening the car door, she passes me the box.

'I think you might need these dear,' she says in her oh so efficient and slightly smug way.

Lillets.

How could I have forgotten THOSE? My cheeks flush hot with a mixture of embarrassment and anger. Both at myself and at Mum for highlighting my oversight in front of Dad. We don't discuss those things openly in front of Dad in our female majority household. Despite being quite young in dress and outlook, they're old fashioned in that respect. We've never discussed sex and periods. If it wasn't for the biology lessons six years ago, I would still believe in the 'gooseberry bush'.

We've got plenty of time before my Dan-Air flight. Or so I thought. Until we hit the A25 bottleneck at Westerham. The traffic crawls; the minutes rapidly ticking away. I curse that the M25 motorway isn't open yet. They started about two years ago but it's going to be years before it's completed. I start to get fidgety and restless, the seat now sticking to my bare legs. No tights for me today. I don't want to be overheating in the sweltering summer heat of the south of France.

My guidebook says the average daytime temperature in August is over 80 degrees Fahrenheit. I've been to Spain quite a few times in August and the climate is very similar, so I guess I know what to expect. My suitcase is stuffed full of t-shirts, shorts, summery dresses and gallons of sun cream. And of course no Lillets. Family friends have told us that sun products are very expensive (and probably sanitary stuff). Well in fact, most things are expensive for us. It's not like Spain, where everything's a bargain. I have 1000 Francs in my purse. It sounds a huge amount but it's only just over 100 pounds. The Cayrols are paying me 200 Francs. So hopefully I'll be ok for the month. I've been saving like mad from my Saturday job at Boots for the last two months. That was when Mrs Neill, our French Literature teacher asked our class if anyone was interested in being an au pair for a month. I thought that Shirley Moffat or Sally Heron would jump at the opportunity, as they are going on to study French and other languages at Uni. Surprisingly they didn't. Although not a naturally gifted linguist or the best student in our class, I love French and the glamour of France. When I told Mum and Dad I'd love to go they said they would put half towards the flight. I had some money in my Post Office savings account, so as they say in French 'Allons-y'.

We finally arrive at Gatwick, by which time the quicks of my nails are bleeding from chewing; I can taste the saltiness of blood on my lips. I am also sweating profusely, despite wearing next to nothing. My Laura Ashley dress is clinging to me in uncomfortable clammy folds of material.

After a trolley dash to the empty Dan-Air check-in, I fling my blue passport and paper ticket at the check-in staff, whilst Dad hauls the suitcase onto the conveyor belt. I'm half expecting them to say check-in's closed. Instead, the attendant smiles at me with her gleaming white teeth and helpfully chirps:

'You're cutting it fine. Check-in closes in two minutes. You need to go straight to boarding gate 53.'

No time for a farewell English cuppa with Mum and Dad. Instead, it's a very rushed 'cheerio' and I'm off sprinting to the departure gate. Past passport control, no stopping at the glittering and tempting Duty Free shops, then along endless white corridors, with their colourful posters which I don't have time to look at. I am weaving in and out of ambling fellow travellers who obviously didn't have to contend with the A25 at Westerham. My handbag and camera are bouncing around my body like puppies in a sack, becoming heavier with every step I take.

I'm surprised that a river of sweat isn't dripping from the bottom of my dress by the time I reach the boarding gate, out of breath and flustered.

People are queuing at the gate to take the bus to our plane. With a sigh of relief, clambering onto the bus, I can finally relax. This wasn't quite how I'd imagined my journey would be. As I climb the stairs of the Dan Air plane, with its slightly grubby white fuselage and red striped livery, I breathe in the smell of the airport; the pungent fumes of diesel and aviation fuel. Not my favourite perfume but tolerable because it promises of a trip to a sunnier, exotic place.

I feel like a proper adult, on this, my first solo flight. I browse through 'Your Flight Guide' but it isn't very exciting. Just flight maps, photos of the crew and adverts. I flit past the very first- 'Celebrate ….a brand new day…with a little gold from Benson & Hedges.' Yuk! Cigarettes. Hate them. It's a disgusting habit which I never adopted after my first drag on Consulates behind the shrubbery years ago, as a third former. Sadly the person next to me doesn't feel that way. He's puffing away on his Duty Frees. The drifting haze of smoke gets up my nose and starts to irritate my contact lenses. Smoking is not my idea of being sociable. I'd ban smoking if I could. I come to the end of the guide. A final advert 'Embassy King Size Filter Extra length. The best in smoking'

Leaving the plane, with the best of smoke in my hair, I step into the intense Montpellier sun. It's like having a hair drier blowing full on at your body. A heat haze shimmers above the ground, below the hot steel of the airplane steps. But at least it's dry heat. I can already feel the sun burning into my pale fair skin, so I hurry in to the cool of the terminal. I feel very proud picking up my rather smart faux leather brown Taurus suitcase with its fashionable buckles and straps. I struggle to get the overloaded case onto the trolley. A rather tasty looking guy comes to my aid. He's a bit old for me though...about 30 something. But when he opens his mouth, I feel slightly wobbly at the knees

'Puis-je vous aider?' he asks in the most gorgeous voice. I accept his help readily, thanking him profusely in my rather shaky French. I've been swotting like mad on some phrases I'll need in everyday conversation but somehow words fail me. I can only manage 'Merci, Monsieur'. We only ever had one hour a week French conversation lessons and they hadn't really prepared me for normal everyday French life. I knew I'd probably have to refer to my Collins Phrase book.

Pushing my clanking, disobedient trolley through to the arrival hall, I am scanning the faces of the families behind the barrier. Which ones are the Cayrols? Then I see a hand written 'Judith Stow' on paper hastily torn from a lined exercise book. I wave at them, and then weave my way through the hordes of travellers in the small terminal. I suddenly feel shy and slightly embarrassed at my rather gauche French as they greet me and then introduce themselves. Bernard is dark and stocky with the start of an early onset middle-aged paunch. Dany is quite pale, slim with an auburn bob. She is the embodiment of French style in a well cut swirl pattern blouse and skirt. The two girls, who I will be looking after for the next month, have wonderful sun kissed tans. Emmanuelle (8), with her long auburn hair, with glints of gold, seems tall for her age. She has a beautiful face, with long curling eyelashes around feline looking brown eyes. Her younger sister, Claire (6) has in contrast, startling platinum blonde hair, as I used to have at her age. Sadly, my hair has become a muddy blonde since becoming a teenager.

We walk to the car park and climb into the spacious Renault, which has seven seats. The girls have been quite shy on the walk back to the car but once in the car they start bombarding me with questions at an alarming speed that I can't follow. Luckily, Bernard speaks very good English and when I flounder, he steps in and translates. Dany is quite shy and retiring and does not say a great deal. She speaks very little English so I will have to make an effort to chat with her.

After a 20 minute ride from Montpellier Airport, through the French countryside with, it seems, predominantly crops of corn on the cob (or so Bernard tells me). There are some rolling hills in the distance, but it's really quite a flat landscape; green interspersed with muddy red uncultivated fields.

Le Cres is a suburb of Montpellier and the Cayrols live on a new estate of very modern sand coloured houses.

I am shepherded through the front door, across the hallway into the heart of the house - the kitchen. It smells of bread, garlic and herbs. Delicious. The tempting lunch is already prepared and laid on the table. They introduce the Spanish-looking Laurence, busy at the ironing board. Her equally Spanish looking daughter, Sophie, who is about two, clings shyly to her legs. It seems like cooking, cleaning and ironing are not my domain. Phew! I had thoughts of being a bit of a skivvy for the month but maybe not. They greet me like an honoured guest.

Through the large sliding patio windows, I catch a glimpse of the garden. They tell me they have only lived in their property for less than a year. There's just a patio and an earthy red-brown patch instead of lawn, with only a few straggly plants and a kennel.

They slide open the window and a very large bouncy friendly dog bounds in to greet me. He's some sort of cross between a setter and a great dane.

'Meet Herisse' waves Bernard with a flourish 'do you know what Herisse means in English?' I shake my head. 'Stream' he says, proudly. Funny name for a dog I think but don't say it. Herisse greets me the only way he knows, with a big sloppy lick. Though, I have since looked up 'Herisse' and it means hirsute or shaggy. I think Bernard's translation skills must have eluded him on that occasion.

Bernard leaves us to manhandle my case out of the back of the car. Dany shows me to my room. They have transformed their study to my temporary bedroom; a comfortable 'put you up' bed and a canvas wardrobe. I'm very happy with my room as it's spacious, newly decorated and has its own toilet and shower. Such luxury.

A knock on the door. It's Bernard with the suitcase.

'I'm sure you would like to unpack your clothes,' Bernard says.

'When you are ready come and have a freshen up drink and some lunch. We all want to meet our English girl. Au revoir pour le moment'. He gives a funny little theatrical mock bow, closing the door behind him.

I unlock my case, take out my rumpled clothes, which I hang neatly in the canvas wardrobe. I place my toiletries on the shelf in the gleaming white-tiled bathroom, then cross the tiled hall to join the Cayrol family in the kitchen.

I think I'm going to have a very good month in Montpellier.

A doodle in my journal

MY LOVE AFFAIR WITH TRAVEL

The seeds of my love affair with foreign travel took root at the impressionable age of eight.

My parents took us on one of the early package holidays with a company called Flair. My very first experience of travelling abroad and flying too. We'd never even taken the ferry across the Channel before.

The small whitewashed Hotel Gili with its' resident bulging-eyed geckos scampering up the walls seemed fantastically exotic. The glistening black cockroaches clicking their bulky shells like castanets against the tiled floors, horrifying.

Yes, Cala Ratjada on the Costa Dorada seemed a different world to the decaying Victorian buildings of Camberwell.

To this day, I can still smell the hot aroma of heady pine and the resin taste it left in the mouth. That was after a walk through beautiful hilly woods under a blisteringly hot sun. My enduring memory is of that trek, with its' tantalising glimpses of the crystalline azure sea through the parched trees and the overwhelming buzzing of the cicadas. For me that assault on my senses was something alien and beautiful; an intoxicating drug.

Overturning my parents' aspirations for me, I shunned teaching or journalism. Instead, the head was over-ruled by the heart. I embarked on a career in the travel industry.

I'd already had a month as an au pair in France. That experience, without a doubt, embedded that pesky travel bug. It was there, wheedling away in my semi-consciousness. Sod the books, let's travel it whispered to my receptive brain. After spending 3 years at University studying English, my passion for travel led me to the 'Toastrack'. This was a rather curious building, part of Manchester Polytechnic. A fantastical piece of architecture. Someone's idea of a breakfast inspired joke. It was one of the only places offering a Postgraduate

Diploma in Tourism Administration. Yet after only two terms, I was off on my travels, much to my parents' veiled disapproval. Although made slightly more palatable by a modest diamond engagement ring on the finger. The result of a brief trip home by Steve and a whirlwind proposal. The lure of both a fiancé and the snowy peaks of the Austrian Ziller valley was far more appealing than the constant drizzle and gloomy northern winter.

That was a ten-month adventure.

Steve, had gone out to Austria with his friend Ian to manage some holiday chalets. They were both German graduates. It took about three months of long distance phone calls to succumb to the temptation. The added pressure of an engagement ring proved too much.

By February 1981, I was on a Dan-Air flight heading to Munich. Venturing out of the airport terminal, I was overwhelmed by the intense white of the snow outside. I had arrived with a totally inadequate wardrobe. I had to make do with some thermal underwear, multiple layers of socks and borrowed cagoule top and matching leggings. Not ideal. Particularly when learning to ski. I have never been so cold and wet in my entire life. I was convinced that I had died and gone to a snowy purgatory during those first few months. Not quite the romantic scenario I had envisioned. Skipping down the green slopes like Julie Andrews in 'A sound of Music'? No definitely not! It was definitely character building stuff. I found myself abandoned on the slopes. My fiancé, Steve and friend Ian had been skiing for months and were very competent skiers. Skiing was now a skill I had to learn on my own. Some lessons wouldn't have gone amiss but that was not possible for a penniless, over-drawn ex-student. After picking myself up off the slopes, brushing the snow off my blue, ridiculously unstylish skiwear, I finally mastered keeping upright and managed not to kill myself.

The engagement was sadly a brief one, melting away as quickly as the Tyrol's end of season slushy snow. By Jan 1982, I was back home, heartbroken again. That was my second great love affair, after my two year teenage romance with Martin, my first boyfriend and first love

The earlier promises of a fairy tale ending were shattered like a fragile mirror. I was left with only a Ratners' 'shabby crap' ring to remind me of my Tyrol fantasy.

Fiance Steve on left, enjoying a chip!

THE JOY OF BRUSSELS IN THE SPRINGTIME

April 2001

We wake up to one of those misty days of great spring promise. The forecast for Brussels looked good too. Sunshine Friday and Saturday and sunshine/cloud on Sunday. I have that feeling in my bones that Brussels will be a revelation.

Our trip to Brussels is courtesy of Brussels Airlines; I was fortunate enough to win the tickets in a competition. I know it sounds ungrateful but I wasn't overly inspired by my prize. I had been to Brussels on a Sabena Airlines trip probably more than 25 years ago. It was on a dull autumn day and we seemed to spend most of the time in a gloomy restaurant just off the Grand Place. Consequently my overall impression of Brussels is dowdy and grey.

On the way to Heathrow we use the perimeter road to avoid the congestion. There's now a track system of 'parking pods' that links the car parking to the terminal. It all looks very space age and a cool way to travel. Rather wish now that we'd gone for the long term parking in favor of valet parking.

However, the Purple Parking works like clock-work even though we arrive early (well worth the £33.00). A cheery blonde lady in her purple livery greets us. I am rather embarrassed by my husband's cheeky patronizing remark:

'I've never handed over the keys to a lady before.'

'Don't worry I'm a professional', she smiled, deliberately ignoring his rather male chauvinistic comment, but winking at me when I pull a face at his political incorrectness.

We have a much appreciated cup of tea in the Tin Duck pub which has interesting décor. Boarding the Avro RJ 100 aircraft is painless. Not like the queuing and scrabbling for seats with some of the low cost carriers. Comfortable seating too, it's a 3 x 2 configuration. We are pleasantly surprised to be offered a drink. Accompanied by a 'Pommeline'; an appley confection which seems to be a cross between a tart and a muffin.

It's brilliant sunshine as our flight touches down on the runway. Our baggage arrives relatively promptly. We make our way down to the Brussels Metro to Brussels Central. We decide to walk from the metro to our hotel- the NH Grand Sablon. It should have taken us about 15 minutes but we take the scenic route (aka the wrong way). The Grand Sablon is definitely the heart of the chocolate and art gallery scene. It's Brussels' equivalent of Mayfair. Our hotel was opposite the Georgio Armani shop and two doors from a Chocoholic shop. Needless to say, Ralph steered me away from both shops. He was more interested in the Belgian beer shops selling all those weird and wonderful flavoured beers. They are not in this up market location but are just off the Grand Place.

The hotel's reception area has something of a Spanish feel to it, not surprising given its pedigree. There's ornate gilded furniture, marble floors and dark wood. The room itself couldn't have been more of a contrast. Stripped wood floors, ultra-modern with lime green décor. Quite an eclectic mix! We are in search of somewhere to eat. Stomachs were rumbling as it was well past lunchtime. We don't go too far – a side road off the Grand Sablon where the clement weather allows us to sit outside, eating Croque Monsieurs and drinking Belgian beer. After a brief stroll, we head back to the hotel for a rest before our pre-booked soiree (20 Euros) at the Music Village:

(www.themusicvillage.com)

This venue offers jazz on Friday and Saturday nights in an intimate club atmosphere with dining optional. The range of food isn't that wide – pasta, pizza or salad but it wasn't too expensive (average 15 Euros) and was tasty. US Saxophonist Bob Mover with the John de Snauert Quartet was on the bill. The advantage with having our meal before the band officially starts, is watching the band 'warm up'. Bob's a great saxophonist. We thoroughly enjoy the session and agree its good value for money.

Brussels, I believe, is best seen on foot. We walk from one end to the other, taking in the Petit Sablon square (very peaceful with fountains), through the largest green area of the Park de Bruxelles, then up to the Botanique where we sit enjoying a beer overlooking the manicured lawns. We can't believe the weather for 24th March, people are wearing their summer clothes. Flip flops and flowing skirts seem to be the order of the day. The Botanique is not, as its name would suggest, a botanical paradise like Kew. Although it has some glasshouses, it's the main building, the Rotunda, which has become the cultural heart of Brussels. I suppose Brussels' equivalent of the Royal Albert Hall. We take a sneaky look in the side door and have a freebie performance. A female singer/pianist is rehearsing. From the bits of French I could decipher I think she's a satirical, comedy artist; maybe a Belgian equivalent of Victoria Wood?

On Sunday after breakfasting in a trendy café just off our square, rubbing shoulders with a newscaster whose name we couldn't remember, we head out to Heysel. This is where the Atomium was built for the World Fair in 1958 attracting over 41 million visitors and taking 58 million hours to construct. This iconic building is still very space age, despite being over 50 years old. We would have had a fantastic view over Brussels if it hadn't been swathed in mist, which no doubt would have burnt off by the afternoon.

If you are very lucky, you might be entertained by the elderly busker just off the Grand Place. He is seated just by the letter box .We sit for probably half an hour watching. There are some road works in progress. There are conveniently placed concrete blocks which provide make shift seating for a gathering audience. It's fantastic entertainment and one of the highlights of my weekend. The bearded guy looks spookily like Uncle Albert from 'Only Fools and Horses'. He was definitely the granddad you would want to invite to your party. If you don't get to see him, – check him out on Youtube. There are a number of video clips uploaded by his fans but I think his version of The Rolling Stones' 'I can't get no Satisfaction' and Eric Clapton's 'Layla' is priceless. He is so happy and full of 'Joie de Vivre', chuckling and interacting suggestively with his audience. It is joyous to watch. It also strengthens my resolve to become a busker. I fully intend to be down Rochester High Street when I retire. I'll be the mad Hooting Nanny in my owl onesy tootling away on my saxophone.

So all in all, Brussels is a delight and an inspiration. I think we will return before long, to enjoy the ambience, the Music Village and of course, catch up with 'Uncle Albert'.

IF YOU WANT TO SEE RAF (PAPY BLUES), THE BEARDY BELGIAN BUSKER, GO TO YOUTUBE. HERE ARE HIS LIVELY VERSIONS OF:

'SATISFACTION'

https://www.youtube.com/watch?v=f9CH60xUViY&list=PL320F09789CA1DFEA&index=39

'LAYLA':
https://www.youtube.com/watch?v=5PJ6IMuv5YE&index=20&list=PL320F09789CA1DFEA

A GREAT CLASSIC BRITISH WEEKEND
(AND A LONG OVERDUE REUNION)

(2nd – 4th February 2013)

During the Halloween week at HRG Worldwide, we have a visit from two witches. They are from Classic British Hotels – a consortium of independently owned hotels. We tentatively enter their "coven" (our Australasia meeting room!). The table is decorated with a disposable cloth adorned with images of pumpkins, black cats and broomsticks; trick or treat tubs of sweeties strategically placed to distract any of the office dieters. The usual paraphernalia of Halloween. The witches give a lively presentation and are assured our attention with a promise of a prize for answering their neatly typed sheet of questions. Some are appropriately Halloween themed too.

I pay attention, ask questions like the dutiful student and hand in my quiz sheet. As we regularly have presentations and some very successful 'Lunch & Learn' sessions, in order to give the suppliers "added value" we are obliged to give online feedback in order to be considered for any prize. Many of my colleagues fall at the last hurdle and fail to give their comments. On the other hand, I love giving hotels my opinion, so the odds of winning something is quite high. I had a trip to Brussels last year and some smaller prize items.

So Classic British Hotels kindly provide me with my final win of 2012 - a night away with dinner bed & breakfast.

We choose the Donnington Valley Hotel & Spa, just outside Newbury. Not too far to travel for a quick weekend away. I also suggest to my daughter, Amelia, who is at Reading University, that she might want to join us to use spa facilities. It sounds ideal.

In fact the choice gets even better. The day prior to our visit my colleague, Josie, makes a suggestion:

'That's not too far from Marlborough. I've been to Marlborough a couple of times. I love it! It has lots of unique designer shops and tea rooms.'

'I've never been there but I do have friends who live in Marlborough' I replied enthusiastically. 'We did attempt a get together three years ago but the World Cup got in the way. Perhaps this could be the right opportunity to pop in to see them? I haven't seen them for thirty years, although we keep in touch with cards and the odd e-mail. I'll ring Jo & Mike tonight. Thanks for that suggestion'.

On arriving home, I make the call only to be disappointed by an answer machine. Undeterred, I leave my message that we'll be visiting Marlborough sometime over the weekend.

The following morning I am busy cleaning the house, much to my husband's chagrin. I can't bear coming back to a messy house, whereas he would leave it like the Mary Celeste, given the half a chance. He is huffing and puffing, shuffling his maps impatiently when the phone rings.

I rush to the handset, fearing it is a cold call but hoping it might be Jo. I recognize her voice straight away. A deliciously soft gentle voice, with only the tiniest hint of a Geordie burr. We agree we would meet up. Finally after all these years....how exciting!

Ralph is not as enamoured with the prospect. He is not Mr Sociable at the best of times and with each passing year is becoming more like Victor Meldrew. I do, however, have to occasionally break out of the insular marital bubble which he would be quite happy to live in.

'Oh don't be such a miserable old Meldrew' I laugh, when he grumbles:

'I was foolish enough to think I would have a quiet, romantic weekend away with my wife. Instead of that you have to populate it with people who I have never met and have no wish to meet'.

He continues his rant from leaving the house until we reach the M25, when he resigns himself to the inevitable thirty year reunion.

The grey uninspiring drizzle miraculously transforms into an almost pleasant day, the nearer we get to Marlborough. We'd agreed to go to their house for 4pm, as Mike was working from home and told Jo that he could finish early. We arrive at Marlborough lunchtime. It is exactly as Josie described it; a lovely market town, with an array of enticing up-market shops if you have a big enough purse.

Marlborough College stands grandly at the far end. Kate Middleton was one of its pupils, I was later told. We walk one end of the town to the other, peering in the shop windows of "Kath Kidston", "Jigsaw", and the other designer shops. However, one small shabby chic shop caught my eye. It has an eclectic mix of gifts, door knobs, paints and a whole cornucopia of household items. It is a veritable Aladin's cave, stacked from floor to ceiling with thousands of pounds of stock. I would have gladly spent a good hour browsing but Ralph was desperate for lunch and hurries me out before I could buy anything. After peering into one pub which seems to be in the middle of a makeover, we opt for the Royal Oak. The sign outside advertises a lunch deal for £5.99. It sounds a bargain and looks comfortable and welcoming. Big squashy leather sofas, very much a Gastro style pub.

We tuck into our club sandwiches, chips and pints of lager with relish. Yes, we know how to live.....even in cultured Marlborough. I brief Ralph again on Jo and Mike, despite having told him numerous times that they are a couple who I knew from my "Toastrack" days in Manchester. I spent two happy terms there as a Postgraduate student, until I was lured to Austria by the promise of fresh air and lots of skiing....and the opportunity to spend quality time with my newly acquired fiancé.

We arrive at their house facing the common, after struggling to find somewhere to park. We aren't impertinent enough to park on their ample driveway. Their home is as I imagined, when writing their address on countless Christmas cards. A large white Georgian house, with tall bushes shielding it from the road. I ring the bell with both excitement and apprehension. I haven't even seen a picture of Jo and Mike in the intervening years. They refuse to bow to the Facebook generation! Jo really hasn't changed at all; still slim and stylish with shoulder length blonde. Just the inevitable wrinkles. We are shepherded from the spacious hall into the equally spacious country-style kitchen. Within minutes, we are both transported back to our early twenties. My memory is flooded with snapshots of our final days as students. It's funny how we all have our own personal memory vaults, yet someone else's recolletions will provide a key to a lost box of flashbacks.

Mike comes bounding in; still the same puppy brown eyes and enthusiasm but his dark brown hair long gone. Just a shiny pate and close cropped grey hair.

Sitting in their elegant, traditional lounge sharing tea and happy memories I was willing the clock's hands to slow down. Sadly on these occasions time evaporates and it seems only minutes before we were leaving. In reality it is 7.30pm and we had a table booked for 8pm at the hotel. Saying our farewells we promise to meet up again soon. I had already caught up with another of our friends, Di, only weeks ago on a very snowy Friday. On that occasion, I almost had to cancel due to the weather but had braved the elements determined that I wouldn't let the opportunity slip by. It's so easy to allow the banalities of life to get in the way of old friendships.

We make our way along the A4 towards Newbury, only half an hour away. On the darkened road we can see a car's hazard warning lights flashing on the other side of the road. We slow in case it was an accident. In our glinting headlight beams we can see the damaged front of a car and a russet fallow deer lying, presumably dead, in the road. We speculate what we would do in that situation. Ring the police to report it? Ralph suggests that no, It would be promptly hauled into the boot. Venison would be certainly be on the menu that night!

We arrive at the hotel, which looks rather non-descript from the outside. A purpose built property, probably constructed in the 70's to fulfil the need for more golf courses with attached accommodation. The reception area is rather bland; just a functional canopy with no signage. Yet walking into the lobby area, it is a different story. Certainly more four star than the entrance promised. Contemporary elegance with huge impressionistic art works on the wall. We hurriedly check in, dropping our baggage into the room and rush to the Wine Press restaurant for our meal. I choose the oriental beef salad and the confit of duck. Chocolate dessert. RB selected the tomato and mozzarella salad with peanut pesto on a bed of spinach. The owner of the hotel, also owns a local vineyard so they are keen to sell the wine. Even for an English wine it is pricey – they want £30 for the cheapest on offer. We have the Chardonnay instead.

It is a very passable meal in this busy 2 Rosette restaurant. It has a pleasant ambience and as far as hotel restaurants go I would say this is one of the better ones. We wander into the bar afterwards. Subdued lighting emphasizes the modern fireplace but because of the low lighting couldn't really see much else. I spy the balcony that overlooks the bar on one side and the restaurant the other.

'Shall we have a look up there?' I suggest.

We sit on the enormous squashy sofa, feeling a bit uncomfortable after our three course pig out. Also bemoaning the fact that we could have had a meal out with Jo & Mike and continued the conversation. Ralph agrees that they are a really lovely couple and that perhaps after all he'd like to get to know them.

Instead, we find ourselves backing on to another couple on the sofa. The romantic ambient lighting seems to be encouraging their amorous passions. We move after a short time, driven away by their embarrassingly noisy snogging.

We head back to our room. Although very fresh, contemporary and comfortable, the décor is a tad bland. Beige coloured wallpaper with a slightly darker beige square pattern. There were a couple of art works but they seemed to be studies in beige too! Fifty shades of beige. I would have been inclined to liven up the walls with a bit of colour. In the beige hallways some of the art works are colourful, brightening up the inoffensive neutrality.

We fall into a contented sleep and slept soundly in the comfortable bed. Well, I sleep well until the early hours and then typically I am wide awake just before dawn. I decide to retreat to the bathroom and read "Human Remains" my latest read from a fellow Mermaid, Elizabeth Haynes. The launch was on Tuesday and Ralph bemoaned the fact that I would have my nose in this new book all weekend. After half an hour (or maybe more) Ralph starts knocking on the bathroom door. He is worried that I'd had a "bit of a turn". He had visions of me lying unconscious on the tiled floor. I return to bed and pretend to sleep instead, just to placate him.

Before breakfast we sample the spa. A very pleasant pool with a sauna, steam room and Jacuzzi. We try to spin out our time, but wrinkled from the water we decide it's time to get dressed and head off for home, with the invariable stops along the way.

We certainly enjoy our Classic British Weekend.

Thank you witches!

THE JOY OF TRIP ADVISOR

Although I am a Facebook user, I only use it intermittently. I find that sometimes it all seems a bit trivial. It can also be such a distraction. You could easily waste hours of otherwise productive time. I have since learnt something even more alarming about Facebook after having attended an excellent "Digital Leaders" 2 day workshop, provided FREE by Social Enterprise Kent. Facebook is constantly trawling data. Not only that, if you have the App on your phone, it is constantly listening to your conversations unless you have changed your "permissions". Facebook really is the Big Brother of the 21st century.

Trip Advisor, on the other hand, is not only an extremely useful tool but also as an amateur travel writer, very fulfilling. It is a great way of giving feedback and creating one's own aide memoire at the same time. I write travel journals but wouldn't necessarily make a note of restaurants and short overnight stays. It's amazing what a wide audience one reaches and quite gratifying to learn that how many people have read one's reviews.

Allegedly over 100,000 readers now!

This is one of the reviews from our Bordeaux to Montpellier trip:

La Muscadelle B&B In Monbazillac

A well-kept single storey building, surrounded by dazzling white gravel, rose and lavender bushes. Very French looking. The owners, Brenda and Mike are very English, so if you want to practice your French probably not the best place. Although for a very warm English welcome you can't beat it. Very comfortable and incredibly clean. I wished we were staying for longer. After dumping our bags in the very white room with its lacy bedcover and chandeliers (my mum would have loved it) we joined our hosts and the other guests for tea on the terrace. We were introduced to Sparky from Santa Barbara, USA. He was on the first leg of his walking trek which would take him through France, Spain and Portugal. Due to the weight of his back pack, he tripped over into a ditch, hurting his back. He literally crawled into the driveway of 'La Muscadelle' unable to get himself upright!

As you can only eat at La Muscadelle with advance notice we headed for nearby Bergerac for dinner.

After dinner in Bergerac we sat at the wrought iron table outside our room. The silhouettes of house martins darting and soaring against the backdrop of sky flecked with salmon, blue and grey. Or the deer scampering through the adjacent vineyard. Chirruping crickets created the early summer's symphonic and hypnotic soundtrack; a truly wonderful chill out location and one can understand why our compatriots abandon the UK for this French idyll.

We paid 83.00 Euros per night including breakfast. Well worth it.

If you want to read any of my other 150+ reviews which I have written since March 2008, I am:

Judith@JudithN474

A JOYOUS RAIN FOREST RAMBLE

February 2018

Singapore, we agreed, had put my surgeon's expertise to the test. I'm impressed with my fully healed 'bionic' leg and ankle, complete with its titanium plates and pins. No swelling on the plane and certainly no complaints from the previously abused limb and its grateful owner. So a big shout out of 'thanks' to Medway Maritime Hospital. OK it might have taken eight hours in A&E to finally get a bed, but let's concentrate on the positive.

It was worth the wait. Now it seems hardly possible that last February I was temporarily disabled, relying on whizzing around in a trusty wheelchair.

What a difference a year makes.

We certainly walked many, many miles in the vibrant, green metropolis of the wonderful city-state of Singapore. Not sure if we covered the whole 50 square miles, of this super modern, fascinating republic but we certainly tried our best. As a new Medway Health Walk leader, I now feel it is my duty to do lots of walking. An aspiring walking role model, even when thousands of miles away from Medway. Although admittedly I didn't take my Medway Health Walks rucksack.

On this short visit, we wanted to do as much on foot, even though at times it is tempting to retreat into the air-conditioned caverns below city level – the excellent MRT – or underground to us Brits. It can be uncomfortably muggy at times but we'll tolerate that for the abundance of sun.

I loved Singapore when we stopped over for three nights ten years ago on our way to Borneo. It just wasn't long enough. This time we had five whole nights. Ultimately, that wasn't long enough either but unless you've got months to spend travelling then five nights is a good compromise. There are certainly bits of Singapore, which are surprisingly 'rain foresty'. Parts of the excellent

Singapore Zoo (https://www.wrs.com.sg/en/singapore-zoo.html) feel like rain forest, which as a self-appointed 'zoo monitor' is, in my opinion, the best zoological garden in the world. You don't have to go all the way to Borneo to get up close and personal to the orang-utans. Here they are free ranging, with only some spikes in the trees in the public areas to stop them coming down to ape their human visitors. Although at four o'clock, they do allow the apes to descend for feeding and to say hallo to their fellow less hairy primate relatives. It was so, so tempting to reach out and touch the mother orang with her adorably cheeky fluffy orange baby, perched within fingertip reach.

The next city rain forest experience has to be the brilliant Singapore Botanic Garden. (https://www.sbg.org.sg/. So much better than Kew and it's FREE, although there is a small charge to enter the orchid garden. We went on Chinese Lunar New Year's Day. It was heaving with people. It would seem that the gardens are one of the biggest draws on public holidays. Not surprising. They say some of the best things in life are free and this certainly is a fantastic example of that. It's so beautiful with lush avenues of tropical trees, bamboos, then open expanses of sweeping lawns and lakes. It was very tranquil the last time we visited but sadly less so on New Year's Day. I had to laugh, though, seeing a local outstretched on a bench, in what looked like an alcoholic stupor.

You could spend a whole day in this magical place but with our limited time, a morning was the most we could allow. We still had to go up the Amazon. The Amazon? Surely, that is South America and the last time I checked Singapore was definitely in Asia. OK, so not the real Amazon, but the River Safari is another part of Singapore Zoo that we didn't have time to see the previous day. We weren't overly impressed with this. A bit too theme parky for our liking.

We took the MRT to our last city Rain Forest ramble in order to conserve some of our energy for the two hour (or more) stroll (http://www.gardensbythebay.com.sg/en.html). The path takes you past a lake, through avenues of bizarre metal structures in Super Tree

Grove. The 'trees' towering up to 50 metres, are gradually changing from metal to a profusion of greenery. In a couple of years over 162,900 plants, consisting of orchids, bromeliads, ferns and other flowering tropical climbers will be transforming the wintry looking branches. Already the plants are up to the top of the structures and

just starting along the branches. We'll have to go back in a few years to marvel at these amazing fabricated trees. We didn't see them at night either, when they are lit up with vibrant colours, all solar powered. Then further along the pathway borders Singapore harbour, where if you are lucky you might catch a glimpse of a sea otter. Sadly we didn't, but the disgusting smell of something seriously rotten caught our attention. Following our noses, we found the culprit. A dead crow, being consumed with relish (not Heinz either) by a three feet long monitor lizard. It's a testament to Singapore's 'greening policy'. It's amazing to have an abundance of wildlife living happily in such a crowded, busy metropolis.

After the free open-air jaunt in this lovely garden, you queue for your ticket to the impressive part of this city garden. The massive eco-friendly domes in the mould of the Eden Project. A profusion of dahlias, orchids, roses,

palms and waterfalls assault your eyes. You can take the lift up to the aerial walkways, marvelling below at the layers of greenery interspersed with radiant colourful blooms. There's a towering pillar of bougainvillea, clematis, hibiscus and ferns, beside you, then below the lush tropical palms and trees. It's a feast for all senses: the assault on the eyes, the wafts of subtle perfumes, be it rose or fungal and then the relaxing sound of trickling cascades. The Gardens by the Bay beside the Iconic Marina Bay Sands Hotel, mainly on reclaimed land, the domes are an architectural triumph of glass, steel and greenery.

The sand of our Singapore travel timer slipped away all too fast. On our sixth day, we were boarding a Silk Air flight to the Malaysian island of Langkawi, a mere hour away. When I say 'island' I should really say archipelago of 99 islands. Most of the other islands are miniscule and don't have jetties, let alone an airport. In fact, before 1986, there was very little in Langkawi, but the Prime Minister at the time decided to give it tax-free status. He'd seen how Thailand had benefitted financially from tourism and was hoping to achieve the same success. It seemed to work but now in parts it's sadly taken on a Disney theme park feel. There's a village with all sorts of distractions and amusements before you board the cable car up over the tropical forest of the Geopark, then an aerial walkway, so you don't get a proper ramble in that rain forest. They also insist you have to have your picture taken, so that you can pretend you were actually in the forest. Despite Ralph's protestations

that we 'didn't want our photo taken as we would not be buying the souvenir picture', they were bordering on dictatorial and wouldn't let us proceed to the cable car unless the photographer took his snap! Despite that, it's a breath-taking view from Sky Cab and the Sky Bridge

....yes everything's themed 'sky'.

http://www.panoramalangkawi.com/.

To get a real feel for the rain forest we signed up for a guided walk with Dev's Adventure Tours

http://www.langkawi-nature.com/.

The minibus picked us up promptly. We introduced ourselves to the very jolly Scandinavian couple (Norwegian but living in Stockholm) and some very academic PhD Belgian students. From our resort, Pantai Tengah to the other end of the island, which is less than an hour as the island is only 25 miles long from North to South and almost similar distance at his widest point from east to west. It seemed shorter than that as we were busily chatting with our very friendly fellow passengers.

We pulled up in the Berjaya Resort's car park. Surely, this isn't it? We were shepherded to the grand open plan lobby of the hotel, where we waited for the hotel's guests (two Americans) to join the tour. Armed with our emergency rations of a bottle of mineral water for the walk, we set off. The first part of our walk seemed to be a guided tour past the luxury-stilted chalets interspersed in the trees or on the beach.

https://www.youtube.com/watch?v=0Jxgf60f3O4

However, we were in fact looking for the spectacled langurs and flying lemurs, which inhabit the trees surrounding the resort. To be honest I'd never heard of a **flying** lemur (colugo). They are an unusual creature in their own species classification and not related to lemurs at all. We managed to catch sight of the slumbering nocturnal creature high up a mahogany tree. After what seemed a while meandering around the resort, we finally enter the jungle. I'm sure 'Dev' has a deal with the Berjaya and his guides are unofficial salesmen!

It became evident very quickly that this was not going to be a 'walk in the park'. It was mountainous terrain on only roughly trodden pathways, clambering over logs then clinging on lianas to negotiate swampy bits. Of course, calamity Judith found the hole sneakily secreted below a pile of leaf litter.

'Aaaah F***' I shrieked, as the similar incident of last year flashed through my mind. However, this time, I heard no crack. Phew! Stuck with my left foot (the rebuilt one) down a hole, I couldn't move. My forever saviour, Ralph, came to my rescue, worry lines etched on his face.

'Are you OK?'

'I think so....just give me a hand and we'll soon find out'

By this time, the rest of the party of trekkers had halted on the narrow track, waiting with anticipation (and perhaps a bit of excitement) to see if there was an injury. One haul and my foot was out of the hole, leaving my walking shoe behind. After a quick assessment, and errant shoe retrieved, we were off trampling the musky earth. Within a few minutes, I had slipped again but forwards, arms windmilling to regain balance. Grabbing a convenient, but sharp, branch helped to stop me falling flat on my face.

'Oh what are you like?' Ralph muttered under his breath, exasperated. Another fortunate near miss with no damage other than a scrape on my palm. Phew, phew!

Less than an hour through trek, the ominous pitter-patter of rain, which then turned into quite a deluge. We, unlike the other trekkers, were somewhat unprepared. A brolly is no use whatsoever on a jungle trek! Before long, we were dripping in our shorts and t-shirts, whilst our companions were dry in their wet weather gear. I suppose the hint should be in **rain** forest, eh? Luckily, it was only for about 15 minutes, by which time we couldn't have been any wetter. Still it is tepid rain and quite pleasantly cooling on our sweaty bodies. We also didn't really think about the end of the walk either. In order to catch glimpses of the nocturnal flying lemur, we trekked in almost pitch darkness. The moon does not penetrate the rain forest canopy! By that stage we were going downhill, which in the dark is worse than going uphill. Of course slippery too after the deluge. The guide had a torch, as did various members of the group and Ralph always takes a torch everywhere. With my affinity with trips and slips, I had the torch and illuminated a safe pathway for Ralph, after I'd found the secure footing. It was quite a relief to be back on the dimly lit, tarmac coated, flat path of the Berjaya resort. Then to cap our adventure, we did actually catch a glimpse of a flying lemur in action. None of our group were quick enough to catch it on film, but the attached clip does the trick!

https://www.youtube.com/watch?v=UAbN1EhOWU8

Needless to say none of my companions had any falls or trips.

Just me.

Oh, the joy of any wood or forest ramble!

The Joy of Sandbanks

September 2018

The HRG Compass Point retirement apartment, if you haven't been there, is in a block of nine flats. The flat itself is very pleasant and quite spacious – two bedrooms (one twin and the double with its own en-suite) Homely, although Christine commented:

'Reminds me of Nan's lounge'.

Sandbanks itself, however, is a rather strange place.

The flat we're staying in, although quite modest, is worth far more than our house. Surrounding us, there are ostentatious gated properties from mock Tudor, regency, to the glitzy glass and chrome or downright hideous....it would appear that anything goes here. The power of money eh?

On our familiarisation circuit of Sandbanks' shady avenues, more sports cars roared past than any other vehicle. Mercedes convertibles and Porsches the commonest "run-around". During this house leering and car spotting exercise, Garry became very excited to see a Zonda Pagani parked outside a fairly low key block of apartments not screened by tall fences or hedges. He whipped out his phone to take a picture.

'What the hell's a Zonda?' I asked.

'Probably the most expensive car on the planet. That would set you back £1.7 ......MILLION !'

'You've got to be kidding me' I retorted.

He immediately showed me this link on google to prove his point:

https://www.jamesedition.com/cars/pagani/huayra/pagani-huayra-for-sale-10090757

Not surprisingly, Lewis Hamilton owns one.

In the secure garage under the apartment, there were only two cars when we arrived....a Volvo convertible and a Porsche. A Ferrari turned up at the weekend but disappears on Monday. I think most of the apartments are holiday homes. In fact, we found number 9 on:

https://www.airbnb.co.uk/rooms/24032109

Apart from two hotels, Rick Stein's restaurant, the Jazz café and some beachfront cafes (Sandbanks' fish and chips price £14.95) there's very little reasonably priced opportunity to eat out. There is, however, a Tesco Express. That was a surprise; I thought they would at least have a Waitrose!

There is very little to do here apart from posing in posh cars (if you have one) or for us plebeians, low cost pursuits like walking, cycling and swimming. Although they do have a table tennis table on the beach. Complete with the bats and ball. I am very impressed with that but only Ralph is willing to play. Not for long though. Far too windy. The ping pong ball had no chance. The clear blue waters look very appealing. I probably would have gone in for a dip what with this Indian summer. I have swum with the penguins in South Africa before. Sadly, I have had cataract and lens implants recently and cannot swim for another month.

We've come to the conclusion that perhaps **most** of these properties are only holiday homes and when their owners are actually "in residence" they have their own staff, order everything on line and never go out.

This is definitely a haven for the rich and no doubt, corrupt. It would be interesting to find on what goes on behind the mysterious electric gates. I wonder how many Sandbanks residents have got away with murder?

The attraction of Sandbanks increases by the day. It was the Bournemouth Arts by the Sea Festival this weekend. Bournemouth is only 15 minutes in the car so stepdaughter, Christine, played chauffeur and we drove in. Loved the festival ...loads of arty things and music. In fact, what's not to love about Bournemouth? We went back Sunday but us oldies walked and the youngsters took the car. To be fair they had Eloise to contend with and we weren't sure whether all the terrain was pushchair friendly.

It's a fantastic walk along the sea line, either on the promenade or on the shore. From Sandbanks to Bournemouth Pier, only takes an hour if you don't dilly dally. The beaches are fantastic...perfect golden sands and kept spotlessly clean.

We caught up with the youngsters at Zig Zag Walkway, which is just a few minutes' walk from the centre of Bournemouth. Eloise was really enjoying her first birthday...asleep in the pushchair.

Ralph was convinced he saw Louise and Jamie Redknapp in the park, during the festival performances. I was going to run back and check. That might have been a bit uncool and I don't know Jamie Redknapp and only vaguely have some recollection of Louise. Might well have been them, as apparently the Redknapps own property on Sandbanks. Garry should have run back with his Canon camera. He's been snapping endless pictures of seagulls and squirrels. He could have made some money with some celebrity pics! Only an hour before Garry stated that the only money to be made selling pictures was for celebrity snaps. He could add paparazzi to his list of many skills. We have nominated him the official photographer but don't rate our chances of seeing the pictures too soon. We still haven't seen their Jamaican wedding photos from 2016. We were optimistic of seeing them at Sandbanks but they aren't on any of the numerous laptops Garry has brought with him. Maybe next time....

Postscript 2019

In 2018 Amex bought HRG for a reported £400m.

We heard at the beginning of the year that the flat in Compass House was being sold.

There are a lot of disappointed retirees. Some have never even had the chance to stay there.

Apparently, Amex, because it is a financial company it is not allowed to hold property as assets. Really?

A JOYFUL STAY IN EDEN

November 2019

It's pitch black but still quite warm but with a bit drizzle outside. I've been sneakily gluing on more eyes to the bird of paradise plants. I did some a few days ago under cover of darkness. Tee hee. It's been my bit of mischief for this holiday.

I'd love to set up a secret camera. It would be such fun to see people's reactions. I'm hoping it's going to create some fake news.

I am going to include the eyes as one of my scenes in the sit com script I am attempting to write. It might be the last scene for the sit com pilot. The end of the story was that I decided to give the very lovely display of 'birds' on reception eyes with eyelashes....at 05.00 in the morning. No one was actually on reception but I suspect they were having a snooze in the back office.

Alas, the receptionist was aware someone was up to no good in their reception area. I was caught redhanded by our favourite and most helpful member of staff, Carmelo. Luckily he thought it was hilarious too and I said it would be our joke, just kept between us and of course Ralph and our new friends, Heather & Dave. Sadly he went off duty at 0700 and his grumpy colleague (or boss) came on duty. When we came back from breakfast at 0800 the whole display had been removed. Ralph said ' I bet Carmelo snitched on you' but I don't think he did. I think one of the humourless guests might have noticed and reported it. However, I have had the last laugh as there are still eyes randomly around the hotel gardens and quite a few adjacent to the restaurant's walkway. I did point them out innocently to the rather dishy young gardener commenting:

'You have a very unusual variety of strelitzia. I have never seen them with eyes before.' He looked at me blankly as he didn't speak much English, so I pointed out the eyes. He was rather bemused at first and then started to laugh. Even the rain didn't wash them off. I don't think the glue is toxic and it's such a small amount I don't think they would come to any harm. The other joke was that I did some with square eyes too. They had obviously been watching too much TV! Needless to say, my long-suffering husband thinks I'm a complete nutcase. But better to have fun with these sort of childish pranks than slip into the vale of despondency eh?

The hotel was delightful despite some of the surly staff. It even had it's own wildlife ....apart from the 'birds'. A litter of feral kittens, who another new German friend, Rita-Marianna, named Adam & Eve and Jesus, Mary & Joseph. Originally she gave them musical names as her cat at home in Cologne is called Amadeus, but then we thought given the Biblical connection and coming up for Christmas, this would be far more appropriate. Ralph filmed The Pied Piper of Eden with her sardines rather than pipes, as the kittens saw me coming with their breakfast and would chase after me! When I get it off his Ipad I shall post on Facebook, as everyone seems to like a cute kitten video. After two weeks of gaining their trust some of them let me stroke them without either running away or hissing at me. They must have been the best fed cats in Tenerife.

THE JOYS OF YOUTH

My Early Treasures

It was a tatty brown cardboard shoebox residing beside the gas fire at Nan & Grandad Morford's house. They only lived next door but one to us, so I could have easily taken some of my toys from home.

Yet inside that box were some of my most treasured possessions. A set of worn black dominos, the white dots barely visible and an eclectic assortment of small items: plastic soldiers, zoo and farmyard animals, metal cars with less than pristine bodywork. I would sit cross-legged on the shabby but clean mat, with its sea of swirling patterns of reds, blues and greens. The dominos would become the farmyard or zoo fence enclosures or the roadways for the cars. The soldiers in their one universal colour would hide behind the domino barricades; their sickly green faces peering over, or some poking their green rifles through a gap.

My four-year-old self would manoeuvre animals, soldiers and cars in my own little fantasy world. I would be engrossed for hours, or until Nanny Morford had done all her chores. Then we would sit up at the worn and scratched yellow Formica table, where she would place the huge book, which I did not have the strength to carry from the corner shelf, just above my treasure box.

This in fact was the ultimate treasure.

'The Golden Treasury of Poetry' actually belonged to my sister, five years my senior. Nan had bought it for her birthday but insisted it stayed at her house. Both Nan and that book directed the course of my life; my love of poetry, illustrations and books originated from that wonderful treasure.

It still holds pride of place on my artist niece's, bookshelf. Holly loves that book too.

I thought it would never be mine.

However, with the wonder of E-Bay I was able to purchase a pre-loved copy. Now it also sits pride of place on my bookshelf.

THE GOLDEN
TREASURY OF
POETRY
Selected and with a commentary by
LOUIS UNTERMEYER
ILLUSTRATED BY JOAN WALSH ANGLUND

CLUBLAND – ACE OF CLUBS

The Walworth Methodist Church had its Bi-Centenary celebrations a number of years ago.

An invitation to the service arrived at short notice. It came from Mary Gee, an old family friend and the daughter of the inspirational Reverend James Butterworth, otherwise known as JB or 'The Head'.

The current Reverend asked me to describe the Clubland I knew as a youngster. What follows forms the basis of my recollections.

JB was responsible for this church or 'Clubland', as we knew it, for 55 years. It was his life's work. This special place was very much part of my formative years and Clublanders are my extended family. The original church was devastated during the London Blitz. The replacement chapel was only rebuilt in the sixties. When I first went there, it was practically new. It is spectacularly stunning in its simplicity. It's definitely a case of 'less is more'. Whitewashed walls meeting a lofty blue ceiling adorned with gold stars and a golden sunrise. The pews and lecterns fashioned in a stylishly plain design in a pale wood. I can remember that wonderful woody smell overwhelming my senses as a young child. No extraneous fanciness - just a simple cross on the altar draped with a cloth that I seem to recall had a motto embroidered into it. Although I have never been a particularly religious person, the chapel enveloped me in a spiritual veil, a breath away from becoming a true believer.

The young Jimmy Butterworth had taken over the church in the Walworth Road before the war. He had come from a poor family in Lancashire and been known as the boy preacher. After the church's destruction, he had a dream to rebuild it with an emphasis on young people. He was definitely a man of mission and vision. He did a fantastic fund raising job in order to build the new premises and that was how Clubland was 'born'. He relentlessly knocked on the doors of the rich and famous for a donation. He even went on a trip to the USA and successfully managed to charm donations from Bob Hope amongst others. There are stones in the courtyard for everyone who donated towards the re-building. The donors then visited the Club over the years, which made it a very exciting place to be. The visitors ranged from royals to artists, musicians, dancers and a multitude of interesting people. Princess Alexandra was a Patron. The old Queen Mary and the Queen Mother also graced the chapel with their regal presence on at least one occasion. Celebrities of the time also visited - the Attenborough family were regulars (including one of my all-time heroes – Sir David).

There was a tradition of excellent drama productions at the club. The theatre and stage were of professional standard.

'Snow White and the Seven Dwarfs' was my first introduction to the Clubland stage when I was about five. I was (not surprisingly) a dwarf.

My sister, Gillian, five years older, was the star of the show. I was quite envious of her pretty costume, when I was in a rather dull coloured outfit of trousers, jacket and belt. The intense lights had both a hypnotic and dazzling effect. The lights were disorientating. I certainly could not see the audience of about two hundred people, including my parents presumably watching us with rapt attention. I remember sitting with the other dwarves at the table with Snow White. Each of us little dwarves had learnt a line. I can't remember what it was now. Probably:

'Hello Snow White, my name's Dozey. '

However, my attention strayed to the bowl of bread adorning the table as a prop. Even though the bread was stale, it was clearly quite a feast for a hungry dwarf. I tucked in with gusto. So busy was I chomping my way through the curly and crispy bread, I forgot my one and only line. My sister was obviously too far to kick me under the table as a reminder I should be speaking and not scoffing!

We enjoyed many other activities over the years. Clubland had wonderful facilities. There were numerous productions in the professional theatre. I remember the well-stocked crafts room where I would regularly complete another work of art to go on the wall at home. The 'green room' also sticks in my mind. Mainly due to its smell. It was the dance room, with padded floors made from pungently smelling rubber. We would prance on the bouncy surface, posing in front of the mirrored walls. On other nights, there would be activities in the gym, including games like British Bulldog, which could get quite rough. I clearly remember Daphne who was in her late teens. She attempted to teach us gymnastics and keep order. I was rather in awe of her. She was tall, slim and had a beautiful platinum blonde bob.

My parents regularly frequented the music room in their earlier years. They both loved singing and were members of the Clubland choir, along with other semi-professional choirs.

Several years later, I was rather impressed with a certain visitor. In my Newsbook, Monday 13th February 1967, I recorded (reproduced here verbatim):

'Yesterday I went to Clubland and went into the chapple and sang hymns then Hayley Mills read all about Jesus hayley Mills ware a fur

coat and I thought she looked very nice. Then we went to get something to eat'

Hayley Mills had been visiting with her family, John Mills, Hayley Bell Mills and Juliet. Although they were seemingly not worthy of a mention.

This picture is from an earlier visit in 1962 by the Mills family.

Hayley is pictured with Mary Butterworth, JB's daughter.

I particularly loved Christmas Eve, as we would go to the Midnight service. My early memories of Christmases are always synonymous with that festive time at Clubland. Afterwards we would go to JB's study for refreshments. JB was a bit of a maverick and was rather fond of the odd glass of wine or sherry. Not quite the normal Methodist line. He would, however, after a party night request that we all took an empty bottle home to put in our dustbins.

The most famous protégée of Clubland, is Maurice Micklewhite Aka Sir Michael Caine. His interest in acting flourished in its nurturing environment. I am sure the theatrical opportunities offered there helped him to secure a place at RADA after leaving the forces.

He did come back to the Club at least once. 'Alfie' and 'The Italian Job' were big hits. He was a star. It was a Thursday club night and my sister met him. She introduced as 'Jim Stow and Topsy Morford's daughter'. My mum and dad had been in numerous theatrical productions with him. Later, in the mid 70's Thames TV contacted my mum. My mum was 'The Organiser'. They asked her if she could get together people who had grown up with Michael/Maurice and would be prepared to be involved in a biopic they were doing. She duly provided various bits of information. The production company asked if they could interview her and some friends in our front room. She wasn't at all keen on that idea and declined their offer. She did, however, provide them with a lot of additional information. Thames TV acknowledged her help in the postproduction biography.

The last time my family performed on the Clubland's stage was in, I think, 1977. There was a production of 'My Fair Lady' and for some reason my dad agreed to play the role of Professor Higgins. My mum and I only had parts in the chorus and helped with the wardrobe but it was great fun. Dad made an admirable attempt at the role. In fact he brought great humour to the part. He had everyone laughing in the aisles when he forgot his lines and chastised the person who was supposed to be prompting. He bellowed into the wings, completely in character:

'What's that you said my man? For goodness sake if you are going to prompt speak up my good fellow!' I always wondered why my dad hadn't followed a theatrical career. He would have been great in comedy films. He had a terrific sense of humour and a good measure of charisma and stage presence.

Sadly, Mum and Dad are no longer with us, but in the past they frequently told us that Clubland was their equivalent of University. It enriched their lives at a time when there would have not been many opportunities for youngsters. They both had interrupted schooling due to the war but Clubland somehow seemed to make up for that deficit. I often dream that they have joined Jimmy Butterworth and his wife, Anna, along with other members, Les and Lilly Harris, Roy and Jean Barrett, Len Dobbs, John Venier, Joyce and Fred Shotter, Ron Boost, Derek Pearsall, Les Bedson and Stan Hewitt. They are all there gathered in that celestial Clubland just beyond our earthly sight. A club which I hope we might one day re-join becoming one big happy family again!

The Butterworths with their Hollywood guest, Bob Hope.

A very young Mary & John Butterworth at the front.

My sister, Gillian, is the pixie at the righthand side at the front. Sadly no pictures in the archives of the "Snow White" production I was in.

Mum and Dad being introduced to Princess Alexandra by JB.

WITH THANKS FOR USE OF PHOTOS AND FOR MORE INFORMATION ON CLUBLAND PLEASE VISIT:

http://jb-clubland.co.uk/

There is also now a biography of Jimmy Butterworth, written by his son John and partner, Jenny Waine: 'The Temple of Youth'.

THE JOY OF HOGS

(HONOR OAK GIRLS SCHOOL)

1970-1977

An excerpt from 'Dum, Mad or Just Plain Blonde'

Written in 2006

When it was time to look at the options for secondary schools, my teacher Mrs Letton made it clear that I should be looking at Grammar schools. My parents were relieved. My sister had gone to Trinity Girls Comprehensive School at the Elephant & Castle and it was not proving a success. They had decided to send her to Trinity School on the advice of her John Ruskin teacher, Mr Pluckrose. He was keen on progressive education and not a supporter of the Grammar School system and said she would struggle. I think mum and dad wished they'd taken that chance, as it looked as though my sister was likely to get an O-Level in shop lifting! She had some very dubious class mates.

We went on a reconnaissance of the local grammar schools – Mary Datchelor in Camberwell and Honor Oak at Peckham Rye. We went to Mary Datchelor first, which was very reminiscent of John Ruskin – Victorian, austere and no open spaces. We then went to Honor Oak and what a difference. Although it was only a little further away on the bus, it was like taking a trip to the countryside.

Honor Oak was surrounded by green – Peckham Rye on one side and the Aquarius Golf course on the other. A huge playing field, tennis courts, a stream running through the grounds and...to top it all....an open air swimming pool. I was sold. This is where I wanted to be for the next 7 years and although I was very sorry to leave John Ruskin, I just couldn't wait to get there.

Hurray. The summer holidays were finally over and I could put on my spanking new blue uniform, blue beret and on 01 September 1970 could head off to my new school. Only Carole Lock, my second cousin, who also lived in Grosvenor Park and I went to Honor Oak from John Ruskin. Needless to say, although we hadn't been really good friends, we were closer for the first few months at Honor Oak, until we found our feet and new sets of friends. One of my first friends at Honor Oak was a shy black girl, called Christine Brown. Christine was a lovely girl but had been at a private school and clearly struggled in a main stream school. Thinking back, I can see she had a lot of dyslexic difficulties. In our first year exams one of the essay titles for the English exam was "The Fog" and she wrote about "The Frog".

In the November of my first term at Honor Oak, we had a major upheaval. During that summer, my parents had decided it was time to get on the property ladder. They didn't want to stay in London (and probably couldn't have afforded to anyway).They started to look in the suburbs and realised we would need to move some considerable distance in order to meet their small budget. We had, during the summer, been to look at new houses at New Ash Green (which I thought were really groovy – they were so modern). Then later houses in Swanley, Darenth, Biggin Hill and finally a 60's built house in Slade Green. Of all the places, from my perspective, Slade Green was the least appealing. It was a drab area, you couldn't see any fields (weren't we supposed to be in the country?) and round the back there was an industrial estate. However, Mum and Dad found a house that was in a pleasant road, had a reasonable sized garden and not a postage stamp, had good sized rooms and was within walking distance from the station and more importantly, that they could afford. It cost £5,000.

My sister had finished her CSEs (and 2 O-levels.... but not in shop lifting) and wasn't going to stay on at school, so there was only the dilemma of my schooling. On considering the options, or should I say option - Erith Grammar School - my mum and dad decided I would be best left at Honor Oak. Erith Grammar was a mixed school and didn't have a particularly brilliant reputation. The local LEA (Bexley) were adamant that I should move to Erith Grammar and put up various obstacles to staying at Honor Oak , including they would not be able to cover my travelling expenses. However, when Mum suggested that they would send me to live with Nanny Morford, who by this time had moved to East Dulwich and was just a walk away from the school, they gave in. I was provided with an annual season ticket and stayed at Honor Oak. I would have been heartbroken to leave there as I just loved it and even in the few short months had made some good friends. Although it was a long journey to school it was worth all the aggravation. Funnily enough I was invariably one of the most punctual pupils. My other good friend, Claire Howard, who only lived up the road would invariably slip in by the skin of her teeth or arrive late.

I really enjoyed having my own bedroom and the other attraction of 87 Alderney Road was that the Dixon family lived next door. On the day we arrived John Dixon came round. He introduced himself very formally:

'Hallo, I'm John Dixon from next door.'

My dad replied : 'Nice to meet you John. I'm Jim and this is my wife Sylvia.'

' I think we'd better keep it on surname terms.' retorted John Dixon.

My parents were a little taken aback by his stuffiness and thought him a bit pompous. It turned out that he was a policeman and was thereafter referred to by Mum and Dad as 'Dixon of Slade Green.'

Despite his formality, I was introduced to his children, Lesley, Andrew and Sarah. It was suggested that I might like to go to Guides with Lesley who was just a year older than I. Lesley was quite a shy and seemingly serious girl but once we started going to Guides together, we became very friendly. In fact she was great fun and we spent quite a lot of time together.....especially in the summer when we would be in each other's houses and gardens. We had great fun re-enacting "It's a Knock Out" in our garden and normally got her brother Andrew doing all the very silly games. He would normally oblige and have us in fits of laughter as he was a natural joker.

When I learnt that the Dixons were moving to Bexleyheath, I was really disappointed, as I thought it might be the end of our friendship. It was a friendship I really valued as I really had no other friend in Slade Green (Aaaah...get out the violins!). I'm pleased to say our friendship survived the move and Lesley and I spent a number of holidays with each other's families and are still friends after 36 years .Admittedly we didn't see each other as regularly as we would liked as she lived in Tanzania for a few years.

My dad at the time worked in the Public Health Department at Goose Green, as a Technical Officer. This was not far from Honor Oak, so in the first year I was there, he would drive to London, drop me off at the school gates and then my mum would get a bus from Goose Green to Covent Garden. I would also get a lift home with my dad but had to get the bus to his office and wait for him to finish. I think I'd sit and do my homework whilst waiting.

Our maths project in the first or second year was fun. It's amazing what you can do with card, elastic bands and the dodecahedron shape...a lampshade! Not sure where I was when these photos were taken – probably swinging from mine! The lampshade finally found its way home and had pride of place for at least a year, hanging in our hallway!

Front Row – Karen Wheels, Christine Brown, Susan Vaughan Back Row – Sarah Morgan, Jackie Gray, Student teacher, Yvette Gordon & Maureen Felton

Front Row – Angela Lang, Susan Tombs, Carole Lock, Wendy Garrett Back Row – Dorinda Perry, Teacher, Margaret Salter & Barbara Burton (I think!)

Once a week I would visit Nan and Granddad Morford's for tea. I became very friendly with Margaret Salter and Sarah Morgan, who also lived in Overhill Road, East Dulwich. Margaret lived at the beginning of the road and Sarah at the end. The large, new, pyramid shaped flats (Dawson Heights) where my grandparents now lived stuck out like a misplaced Egyptian memorial in the middle of this residential road of mainly 1930's built properties. My Grandparents moved into their very chic split level flat when this council estate was built. Their flat was lovely and they had the most fantastic view of London as the estate was right on the top of the hill. The downside was that although most of the residents were fine there were the some shady elements. I remember a friend leaving their bike outside for only a few minutes and having the lights pinched. My nan's comment was that there were a few people living there that would 'Steal your eyebrows given half the chance'.

When we were in I think the 2nd year, Sarah decided to have a party at her house. Her parents were very liberal and quite happy to have a gaggle of teenagers come round in their absence. I seem to remember half the class being there. However, we were not all agreed on our tastes in music and when someone had brought a David Cassidy and a Donny Osmond LP and insisted on playing it, Sarah, Margaret and I scarpered upstairs. We were not into the "Puppy Love" scene and would rather have had pins stuck in our eyes than listen to that puke making stuff. We were into Led Zeppelin, David Bowie, Lou Reed, James Taylor and Leo Sayer. Poles apart! We also thought we were really sophisticated and into meditation and the "occult" etc. and decided we would go upstairs and meditate. It was round about this time that Sarah, Margaret and I had been dabbling with an Ouija board round at Sarah's house and had a very weird experience. Needless to say we had ended up scaring ourselves.

I must say that I was starting to feel that the party was not really that much fun and whilst in a middle of some weird incantation a little thought slipped into my mind – 'I wish something exciting would happen.'

Within minutes, we heard screaming. Blimey, my telepathy worked! We raced downstairs to find out what was happening. The girls were shrieking and cowering behind chairs. 'There's a strange man leering through the window' they screamed hysterically. We thought we'd better go outside and investigate. There on the doorstep was the 'strange man'. Margaret's dad! He'd walked along the road to collect her as he didn't want her to walk home by herself in the dark. Margaret was mortified. Still it did spice up the evening.

Caroline's (Bruce/New) recollections of our school days:

"I recall from memory: Beverly Nicholls, Terrie Currie, Judith Stow, Sarah Morgan, Margaret Salter, Penny Charles, Maureen Felton, Barbara Burton, Yvette Gordon, Christine Brown, Louise Geritty, Susan Moore, Dorinda Perry, Janice Tillyer, Claire Howard, Sandra Green, Susan Tombs, Deena Clarke, Wendy Garrett, Andrea Hodges, Jackie Grey, Susan Vaughn, Sharon Lovell, Karen Wheels, Carole Locke, and Carmel Heffernan & Sara Fung.

Who remembers jumping the stream and all those dead birds on the hockey pitch?

Teachers: Mrs Andrews, Miss Brace, Miss Parsons, Miss Holl, Mrs Terry, Miss Stuart, Mr Morpurgo. Miss Willis, then Miss Bayliss - the Heads. Premises Wheeler & Miss Tyler. Who was our music teacher, the angry Scotsman? Lunchtime discos, dancing to 70's music such as Lieutenant Pidgeon's "mouldy old dough" (those 4 opening notes!!)

The angry Scotsman was Mr Cook and I remember he was a bit weird. He used to threaten us with a belt that he said was in his case. He even gave it a name (possibly "Bessie") and said we should behave otherwise he would get it out. Or perhaps he wasn't talking about the fictitious belt at all. I think he was a bit of a sad case, suffering with SMS (Small Man Syndrome)

More of Caroline's memories:

of the day trip to Boulogne (I think she meant Le Touquet):

"I accidentally broke a ship made out of shells and scampered but Anne didn't, or was caught so had to return to furious shopkeeper and pay for the damage.

That's when I realised Anne was different. Chris would have run too."

Our French Lessons:

Remember Miss Holl's enormous bosom and this song...

'Dans la foret lointaine

entende de la cuckoo,

Il responde hibou,

CUCKOO! HIBOU!

We used to have to sing that minging song every lesson in year 1F."

....

MISS HOLL our French mistress and form teacher: I have 2 hysterical memories of her and Christina!!

Christina and I were frenzied about each other in 1F. Monstrous soul mates who talked incessantly in class and then on the phone after school! Pre - adolescent and like twins in mind and spirit.

We sat together on the right column of seats, me near the window overlooking the quadrangle. Front/middle position.

Once, Christina sneezed suddenly and dived under her desk to blow her nose - too polite to mess with it in full view.

MISS HOLL WENT MAD. She gave Chris an Order Mark! The first one in our whole year. Chris burst into tears and then said: Thank- You Miss Holl... I was stunned. I would have died on the spot or runaway and killed myself. Instead, Chris stood up and reported herself and the Order Mark to Miss Willis, along the corridor. The class went silent in their condemnation of this bad girl and their House Team Ashley, losing 4 Good work Marks!!

Then I remember another incident. Christina regularly brought sweets and comics to school from her dad's shop in Crystal Palace Road.

Once, during Holl's boring French lesson, she was caught reading an American Superhero magazine and scoffing chocolate.

Miss Holl snatched those priceless items, confiscaing the articles forever.

Chris jumped out of her skin but was furious!! She was strong willed and no one snatched her stuff!

She shouted: "Miss Holl! You will return my property!"

When Holl recovered from the shock of this retort from a mere pipsqueak, she stuttered a refusal - whereupon Chris bellowed: "Well then Miss Holl - You owe me one shilling!"

The class was horrified and expected expulsion...time stood still... there was probably another Order Mark but I was in shock... Chris was a true heroine in my eyes and can do no wrong since!

Lastly Caroline's embarrassing summer dress and the ignominy of no chest:

"I have a really embarrassing recollection of you and ME...

*My "seamstress" mum made me an Honor Oak dress using a pattern given to us by a f******g wildebeest bosomed pupil.*

Consequently, the armpits were gigantic circles - allowing one to gaze straight through to the quadrangle on the other side.

I bravely tried to cover up this oversight by wearing my jumper in a 40 degree heatwave, in the hope that I'd GROW into it as mother had intended. (Still waiting).

Beverley Nicholls sniggered endlessly one lesson, when I rashly forgot to camouflage my baggy dress and pointed out that not only could you see right through the arm holes but there were NO TITS attached to my chest either!!

Well, Anne Schuster took up the hue and cry and taunted me endlessly during P.E. afterwards; making squirming into and out of clothes, without revealing my androgyny, a feat of true athleticism.

To this day she denies it, the cow. But being paired up with Miss Bustline of Britain was a pain thereafter - especially at the open air swimming baths in Bellingham - where she bounced around on the springboard, executing perfect little dives and lazing around the poolside with Olive Oyl (me) in freakish attendance. Aged 12 etc."

I loved attending Honor Oak. With such lively school friends, who wouldn't have fun? The only problem was that sometimes I thought I was there primarily for socialising and having fun rather than there to learn. In my second and third years I did go through a patch of not very good reports and my parents threatened to move me to Erith Grammar School if my behaviour didn't improve.

Admittedly in the second year I hadn't been very well behaved. Particularly when I became very friendly with Susan Moor. Susan was a mischievous, lively and often quite naughty girl. It doesn't take much to lead me astray.....

One day things got particularly out of hand in the biology lesson with Mr Morpurgo (or was it physics and Chemistry? He taught all three) who we often led a merry dance. Mr Morpurgo was an Austrian who despite having lived in this country nearly all his life had a very strong accent. "Now girlz" he would shout over the rising din of 28 jabbering girls, who he clearly could not control. He was a bachelor who lived with his mother and owned a pet tortoise. We could waste a whole lesson just getting him to tell us about his tortoise. Need I say more?

However, he really lost his rag when Susan and I decided to lead our table in a bit of group singing. He was furious and shouting for us to

'Stop girlz' and decided that the best thing to do was split Susan and I up. We had been sitting at the back of the class. He put Susan at the front. I decided that perhaps enough was enough and got on with the work we were supposed to be doing. However, Susan decided more (pardon the pun) singing was in order and started the front table off.

This launched Mr Morpurgo into a frenzy and he stormed over to Susan and grabbed her by the hair and dragged her across the room with stool attached as her legs were wound round the stool. We were stunned into silence. Susan was screaming in agony and when he finally let go she ran out of the classroom crying. It turned out he'd pulled a huge chunk of hair out – she had a bald spot. I can't remember exactly what had happened after this but I think Susan had a reprimand from the Head, Miss Willis. Mr Morpurgo was sent home with an even bigger reprimand. He did come back to school though. These days he would no doubt be dismissed and probably prosecuted for assault!

Anne Schuster (Humphreys) has provided me with all her recollections and you will notice her version of events is much more toned down:

'After rigorous interviewing (we all got in) and lying about the books we loved to read (CS Lewis and JR Tolkien rather than Bunty, Tina and Dandy), we had to do an extensive project, collecting pictures of plants and animals and categorise them into genus over the summer holidays. I can remember Julie and I tearing our hair out at her house and debating what a sea slug would come under!

On the first day, our hemline above the knee was checked (no more than 3 inches, and then the older girls 'christened' our berets by plucking the middle out. I got an order mark that first year for eating in school uniform.

I have very few negative memories, and remember having a very close knit set of pals from about the 2nd year onwards, although allegiances changed from time to time.

Running all the way through was my friendship with Julie Hutchins who I would walk to school with often carrying far too much and the occasional instrument (Trombone for me and French Horn for her) but more often a heavy bag and (after hockey practice) a hockey stick to ward off muggers on the Eddystone Bridge near the crematorium at Brenchley Gardens, Forest Hill.

Caroline and I were occasionally quite evil and remember mischievously pushing Julie into the waves on Folkestone beach (in November!). She was only supposed to get her feet wet but fell in properly, so it was then a joint effort to disguise the fact from a disapproving Ms's Andrews and Allsop. We all donated an item of clothing to keep her warm until we got to the coach. It was me who had to face her Mum Lillian who was 'very surprised at me' and gave me an earful!

We (Caroline and I) were also responsible for nearly breaking poor Alison's nose whilst playing a party game at her Birthday party (I think we would have been 12 or so) by pushing her face into the flour pie that she was picking a sweet from. It had seemed Innocently mischievous – until we saw the blood!

Oh, and then there was the time that we wrapped Caroline (a willing participant in a big blackout curtain in 4Z) and twizzled her around so eventually she could not escape and as she protested loudly as her hair began to rip out but we laughed. The teacher Mrs Andrews walked in (face like thunder) telling us all off, especially Caroline – who happened to be form prefect that term. We were ordered to vote again and see if she should retain her position! Luckily Caroline's many friends re – voted her in her favour...

I fell out of favour once again with Mrs Andrews when I was caught smoking (peer pressure of those who would label you 'chicken' if you didn't) in the loos. I only got caught once (smoking menthol ciggies -Yuk!) – a great relief since it was the perfect excuse never to do it again!

There's my confessions out the way!

Julie once got hit in the face in hockey which nearly knocked a tooth out, and I remember walking with her holding it in to her dentist to have it fixed back in. She has trotted round the world with her doctor hubbie and 3 children and currently lives near Sydney Australia.

My Dad used to call the 'gang' in the second year the second year mafia – we gave an impression I think of loud and rude when we were out, and can remember us hanging out of Dad's taxi window shouting mild (but lewd) comments to boys. The mafia included at the time (I think) Caroline, Julie, Anne, Janice, Clare, Penny, Alison and Terrie.

It was about the same time as my elder sister Jenny dubbed us 'Frosty Bums', because the length of our skirts rose faster than the length of our legs steadily from the second year onwards.

I also remember a day trip to France during the First year. We went by coach with Miss Holl. She taught us French songs and gave us a test every week, with a small black and white picture torn from a calendar if we got 10/10.

I also remember a good few geography field trips – Box Hill, Shoreham Valley, and the best – Malham Tarn. I fell in love with the place and the people, but it was many years before I got to revisit it. We now go practically every year.

On the trip we walked and climbed, scrambled down scree banks, crawled in caves and walked along freezing river beds. The accommodation was basic but like being in an Enid Blyton book with a 'dorm', midnight feasts, and sneaking out to play football in the dark. I remember running the bath and there being fresh water shrimp coming out the taps! Julie was peeved all the holiday as she had brought a little bottle of Gin which had fallen from her pocket onto the track as we got off the train. We hoarded Kendle mint cake, and took flow readings in freezing streams. It was March and it snowed – the landscape was beautiful.

Equally good was the Biology field trip to Wales to Dale Fort – we bonded on many a windswept and cold beach!!! We collected samples from a muddy river estuary, using a wire grid and got filthy!

People

All the girls in my class were well remembered:

***Julie Hutchins** A girl on a mission to go into the medical profession – chanted Latin verbs to me walking home and won the best raspberry competition. The Prize.... Free French horn lessons! Right Julie as Goldirocks. Left:*

Left -Retaliating in a water fight on the hockey field. Julie & Anne Schuster.

***Caroline Bruce** went to work for Southwark Council Architects Dept. after school and now lives with her hubbie and 6 kids aged 14 – 24 in Kettering, Northants*

Right Caroline, Julie Anne. Wendy and Terrie.

***Sharon Lovell** was a really nice girl- was responsible for the school rules getting tougher about jumping the stream after she broke a leg! Very tall and elegant! Now training to be a priest.*

***Yvette Gordon + Barbara Burton** inseparable friends, who were really nice company. Barbara was a great athlete and brilliant sprinter- shocked Miss Wheeler with her astounding 100 yards sprint across the playing field - which was close to an Olympic record. Yvette was a great hockey player.*

***Susan Vaughan** – I remember her deep interest in Biology extending to burying a rat in the grounds to decompose so the skeleton could be retrieved for the interest value with the full support of Mrs Terry our marvellous Biology teacher*

***Sandra Green, Susan Tombs and Karen Wheels and Carole Lock** – way ahead of the rest of us with their grown – up appearance, experience of life and general demure sophistication and proper hair-do's.*

***Christina Joslin** – a tour de force. Forthright and willing to debate anything, speaking her mind, throwing out compliments or opinions equally willingly. Typical red- head. She is on the right of this beach shot with Caroline and Sandra.*

***Janice Tillyer –** Another giggler, well liked and quite organised mixed with ditzy and would hold down 2 or 3 jobs whilst still at school.*

Photo: top: Janice Tillyer, Anne Schuster, Alison, Karen Wheels, Susan Tombs, and Carole Lock. Bottom: Clare Howard, Julie Hutchins, Terrie Curry, Sandra Green, Christina Joslin, Caroline Bruce. Judith quite possibly taking the photo.

Terrie Curry – *a shining light from day one – probably the most popular girl in the class – giggl*

y fun personality, generous to a fault, and beautiful with the biggest blue eyes and long blond hair, and the tiniest waist possible! Terrifically artistic and an imagination and skill in writing that was a real talent. Still lives near the school- has 5 children and a passion for Salsa.

Alison Bryant – *A very sensible girl with a wicked (and I mean wicked) sense of humour. Always managed never to have a hair out of place and a style beyond her years. We bonded in mutual confusion when we decided to take A level Maths and often needed to help each other in class and for the homework. Has 2 grown up boys and lives in West Norwood.*

Claire Howard - *lovely personality, a real giggler – kept us on the straight and narrow more than once. Now living in Tonbridge Wells with 2 grown up kids.*

Christine Brown *always had such neat clothes and hair! She was a terrific cook in D.S.*

Susan Moor *– fabulous swimmer, hockey and netball player famous for her run in with Mr Morpurgo, iwho when he wasn't being strayed from chemistry by being encouraged to talk about his pet tortoise was being taunted by certain students who found Science boring. On one occasion Susan pushed him too far and the rest is history.*

Angela Lang and Beverley Nicholls

I was in awe of them in primary school seeming to be way ahead of their years then and wearing the trendiest clothes. So by about the second year they seemed fully grown up and living a different kind of life to us mere mortals. Angela lives Shirley, Croydon. She has 4 children and 1 grandchild, and in still keeps in contact with Alison. Beverly now lives in Queensland, Australia and has 3 children and 2 grandchildren called Jade and summer.

a bit of Judith's artwork.

Wonky view from the science block!

Dorinda Perry *- Another of the 'grown up set'. I liked her tremendously – really self-confident- fell hopelessly in love with a Turkish boy and went to Turkey to get married at about 15. I can remember us all worrying about this and Mrs Andrews trying to persuade her to wait until she was a bit older, and to finish school first. She is on the far left top of picture.*

Louise Gerrity *– very sporty (swimmer) as a teenager, nurtures her artistic side after leaving school. I was close friends with her when I started at HOGS because she lived in the same road and her Dad would often take us to school. There are unconfirmed reports that she may have passed away.*

Right: Dorinda and Louise

Andy Hodges *– A lovely girl, with thick blond hair and a wide experience of different places.*

Penny Charles *– A real trouper, coped with everything life chucked at her, was the most organised person I will ever meet. e needed a spare anything, a paracetamol or even needle and thread, Penny would have it in her bag like Mary Poppins. Now lives an idyllic rural life in Canterbury Kent.*

Judith Stow *– always good for a laugh – very artistic, went into tourism, and later went on to run the local Dyslexia association in North Kent.*

Deena Clark – nice girl – had a nutty dog and lived near Ivydale Rd

Maureen Felton *– A loner - preferred her dogs to people I think. I regret not getting to know her.*

Wendy Garrett *part of the Nunhead set – always got on well with her – now working with the forces in Afghanistan – hope she stays safe.*

Margaret Salter *very sensible, best friends with* ***Sarah Morgan*** *and great gals. Sarah works for the DVLC in Wales and has a show garden But her children have taken a career in acting and have been on the TV. Margaret is a TA and has 2 young boys that keep her on her toes!*

From Top Left to right Sycamore, Karen, Anne Schuster, Alison, Clare, Sue, Chris Brown, Christina Janice Tillyer Caroline, Sharon, Penny, Sarah and Margaret

***Anne Sycamore** – another sensible head with a great sense of fun has a 6 year old boy and lives in Kilkenny, Ireland. (Right)*

***Jackie Gray** - sweet girl at school – one of those I walked home with -*

Now Lives in West Sussex

***Deborah Rawson** – talented dancer and actress. A beautiful girl.She became a professional dancer, then dance teacher. Now lives in Gloucester*

***Rachel O'Neill** – another drama talent and lovely girl.*

***Anne Woods** – Thoroughly nice, friendly personality - became a teacher. Left – Anne is between Anne Sycamore and Anne Schuster both with bones in hair.*

***Lucy and Caroline Wright** – 2 triplets who were probably the brightest in the school and always came first or second in class!*

***Nandita Argowal** – lovely girl, very quiet.*

Julie and Nandita

***Aruna Patel** – a giggler and a good listener – also worked with her in Littlewoods on a Saturday and walked to school with her. A great friend to have. Now lives in Amsterdam with her husband, an artist.*

***Lynne Robertson** – had a lovely smile and sunny disposition*

Julie Rosomon** – joined the 6th form - very arty and quite grown up for her age **Jo Havelock

Cynthia Douglas. Studied A Level art with me, hence this pastel drawing. She drew me but I don't suppose she's kept her drawing for 45 years!

Left: Sarah Fung who was half Chinese and into T. Rex.

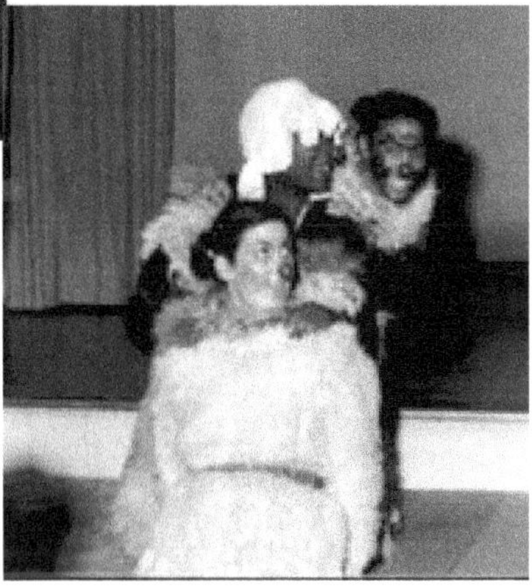

Right: Yvette Chandler, Cynthia and Christine in Goldirocks and the 3 bearosauruses

Ch

re

comic personality, became best friends with Julie. Went into the Police force. She had a real talent for imitation and a wicked sense of humour – also taught for a while then started own business.

Cynthia Douglas by Judith

Anne Schuster *I left school and trained to be a Building Surveyor. I did this for 20 years (mainly in Maidstone, Kent), then had a child -Joanne who is now 11. I then changed to teaching Construction, first at the local FE College and more recently under 16's within and partnered with local schools. I married John (yes the same one with the motorbike and long hair) about 3 years ago. We live in Gravesend and he still has motorbikes.*

<u>What did HOGS do for me? By Anne Schuster (now Humphreys)</u>

Honor Oak extended my self-belief encouraged me to be independent, think for myself and follow my own path, to question all I was told.

I think we all felt quite privileged to have such a quality of teaching in exceptional surroundings. Most of us came from very ordinary backgrounds which once you scratched the surface were in fact in some cases quite extraordinary, full of family difficulties, internal turmoil and dark secrets that never made it past the school gate. We were always kept very busy and occupied in and out of school and some days it was a haven for us to just come to school and enjoy the camaraderie. I feel very lucky to have been a part of that, we suffered the O and A levels together and a bond was made that will never be broken even if we see each other every week, year or 31 years!!!!

Apologies to anyone I have missed out!!! "

I also remember Susan and me getting into a contretemps one day when we were jumping the stream. This was a favourite pastime during the lunch breaks. I can't remember what it was all about but it ended up with us having a bit of a fisticuffs and falling in the stream and getting absolutely soaked from head to toe. Jumping the stream was OK (or at least it was until Sharon Lovell broke her leg) but getting wet was an absolute no-no. I remember Susan and I being hauled up in front of Miss Willis and getting a right ticking off. We left two muddy puddles on her lovely carpet though so we didn't mind too much.

Christina (Joslin) looking wistful on one of the bridges over the stream. Get the boots though….they were the height of chic - platforms!

About the same time (I think) I had a fight with Beverley Nicholls. Beverley and Angela Lang were mature girls and seemed very confident and self-assured. I think most of the class were in awe of them. One day Beverley started picking on Margaret Salter. Margaret tried to ignore her but was obviously getting upset and would not retaliate. I couldn't stand by and see one of my mates being bullied, so of course I had to retaliate on her behalf and Beverly and I had a slanging match. I made reference to her "spider eyes" (she wore lots of mascara) amongst other things which she didn't like and then she came over and shoved me saying "who are you calling spider eyes". I shoved her back and then before we knew it we were having a full scale cat fight, pulling hair, scratching, kicking.... the lot! I think I got the better of her physically although I seem to remember my glasses getting broken. Of course I didn't tell my parents how that came about! Beverley now lives in Australia, where my second cousin Carole Lock told me she visited her about 10 years ago.

Susan Moor left I think in the third year when her family moved to Basingstoke. There is an entry for her on friends reunited and I intend to get back in contact with her. Although Susan and I became very friendly, she had always been best friends with Louise Gerrity. They both were at the same primary school – Stillness – and heavily involved with competitive swimming. Louise was a likeable, really fun lively girl. Sadly Anne Schuster saw her a few years ago at a bus stop and she was clearly on drugs. Subsequently we have heard rumours that she died of a drug overdose but nobody has properly substantiated this.

I had various other close friends over the years. Penny Charles and I were very friendly right up into the fifth year and also Anne Sycamore. One holiday Anne and I had an ongoing correspondence which was very funny and ended up with mailing talcum powder in the post. She had a very good sense of humour. We are now in touch spasmodically via e-mail as she lives in Ireland.

The second year stands out in my mind as we had a student English teacher, Mr Brown who was absolutely gorgeous and I think the whole form were in love with him. Thinking back, he probably wasn't really that gorgeous, it's just that we only had a handful of male teachers, who had clearly been beamed to our school from either the Planet Ugly or Planet Smelly, or were offspring of alien alliances from both. Mr Jenkins was a prime example. Wild ginger hair, glasses, tatty corduroy jacket, yellow fingers, yellow teeth, and with a breath to die from... Urghhhh. Yes, so Mr Brown was definitely a breath of fresh air. It must have been very difficult for a young man having to control a bunch of girls who were clearly quite hormonal by this stage. In fact some girls were hormonal before they left primary school (I won't mention any names they know who they are!). I remember being reprimanded by Mr Brown after we had a sponsored skip at lunchtime and arrived in class very dishevelled and shirts unbuttoned to the navel. We definitely liked to be provocative.The funny thing about this short episode was that both Sarah and Margaret became a bit obsessive about him and started to stalk him and even went as far as supposedly finding out his address and standing outside his house in the hope of seeing him!.

Recollections from Anne Sycamore

'I was on the scene when Sharon Lovell jumped the stream and broke her leg. I remember Miss Wheeler, (she of the ice blue eyes), picking her up and carrying her across the sixth form lawn to the office. I also remember you and Susan Moor taking it in turns to forget your sewing bags to wind up the teacher. Can't remember her maiden name (Miss Lunt?) but she got married to a foreigner, and can't remember her married name either!!!! Memorable character.

Mr Cooke, the music teacher, was a dab hand at hurling a chalkboard wiper at people across the music room. I remember a comment he made on my report one year – "I doubt Anne has ever made reference to the copious notes that she has been given through the year".

As you can guess, I enjoyed belting out a tune vocally, but was never much cop at the theory side.

I think I can count on the fingers of one hand the number of times I swam in the school pool, even when it was covered. I do recall a swimming gala one year when it was uncovered, and the spectators sat on the grass round the outside. There was a diving competition and Christine Brown was a competitor for the standing dive from the edge of the pool. The idea was to start from a rod-straight position with the arms above the head and just hop off the edge of the pool, entering the water gracefully feet first with as little splash as possible. We can commend Christine for her perfect execution of this, and we all applauded, however the applause died to a ripple as she took rather a long time to return to the surface. So long, in fact, that Miss Wheeler, (her again of the ice blue eyes), started making her way to the edge of the pool with her hands on her buttons in case she needed to strip off and dive in for a rescue. As we held our breath, so did Christine, and she finally emerged fingernails first, still in exactly the same pose as she had entered the water, after having gently sunk to the bottom and then gently pushed back up again. Louise Gerrity and Susan Moor were members of a local swim club, and made everyone else look like a drowning rat in the water. They had very shiny hair from regular immersion in chlorinated water.

Did anyone else ever search for golf balls in the shrubbery that had been hit over from the course next door? My brother-in-law's Dad used to pay me 5p for each one I brought home, as he would take them out for practice and not worry about losing them. Occasionally, I found an upmarket one that was in good nick and he would give me 50p for them.

Hands up everyone that did or may have considered having a fag in the shrubbery? Hands up all those who smoked "Consulate" menthol cigarettes and thought they were cool? UUUUGGGGHHHH!!!! What were we thinking!?!?! Fags were bad enough, but menthol.......!?!?"

Don't forget Miss Todryk of the Prince of Pagodas fame. She introduced us to volleyball and we'd hurtle into the dining room at 1.05 and be fed and in the hall ready to play by 1.15. How we ever got past the half hour without searing indigestion I don't know! Barbara Burton, Yvette Gordon and Christine Brown were always there. Christine was great at getting the ball away without ruining her beautiful nails. Did I tell you she was working in Barclays Bank at Lewisham during my last couple of years there?

Does anyone remember the time I found a porno novel on the P4 bus and brought it into school? I can't remember where we hid it in class Z, but we would hide behind the curtain at lunch time and someone would volunteer to read a bit out loud while someone else kept an ear out for anyone coming into the room.

When Mrs Andrews the geography teacher left we were all convinced she was pregnant because of those awful tunic tops she wore.

Lining up to get the hockey sticks in the sports shed. Lovely smell of creosote in there. Once or twice during summer games we actually got around to throwing discus and javelin. If anyone had a talent it was never going to be found when you only got to having a go once in the school year!!

Terrie and someone else tried to make stink bombs and left a jar of something nasty in one of the room Z cupboards.

The school hymn – "We rest on thee, our shield and our defender..." I can't remember any more of the words, but every time I hear Finland it always brings a lump to my throat. (Sniff)"

I don't remember that about the needlework bags - was that why Miss Ramsden (latterly Mrs Muir) hated me so much!!!! I hate needlework...and I remember I did really well in the needlework exam and she accused me of cheating. I was furious. Anne was wrongly maligning Miss Lunt who to my recollection was a very nice lady – I think she taught biology? (Answers on a postcard please.....)

I have to put my hand up to the Consulate cigarettes in the shrubbery though. Probably did me a favour as I think it put me off cigarettes for life!

And further thoughts from Julie Hutchins (I think)

'I only went to two parties, and one of them was at Penny Charles', where her "mystic" Mum wafted in and out saying how lovely it was to see her friends from school and we should come more often. I can't even remember who else was there. The other was Anne's party, (the one where we were taken home in the taxi yelling out of the window) at which I felt really foxy because my Mum had made me a pair of brown velvet (!) hot pants with bib and cross straps (!!) which I wore with American Tan tights (!!!) and a pair of white patent court shoes with Cuban heels (!!!!) and laces that wrapped up to the knees (!!!!!!!!). I think this was just before I decided fashion was not something that came to me naturally, so I gave up.

Anne Sycamore's (Matthews) e-mail to me:

"Dear Author,

I look forward to receiving information on purchasing your tome when completed. I hope you will include some remembrances of the Sixth Form Xmas Plays that were a feature much anticipated throughout the school as the Yuletide approached each year. If you would wish this to include the photographic record I have of "Goldirocks and the Three Bearasauros'", as performed by the class of 76/77, please let

me know and I will forward these to you. They are on the FR website but I don't know if you can download them from there. If you feel this is best left in the vaults of time then, so be it. Does anyone remember who lobbed the window hook out the window from the first floor and into the roof of a teacher's car parked underneath? Of course, we all remember Sharon Lovell breaking her leg while jumping the stream, and the state of the swimming pool in autumn when the leaves began to fall. What about the lovely smell of creosote in the sports shed and the rush to get the best hockey sticks? Barbara Burton ran the 100 metres in about 13 seconds and made the rest of us look like snails. Barbara accidentally hit Yvette Gordon in the face with a hockey stick during a game and broke her glasses. The poor girl was distraught that she'd damaged her best friend. What about all those sixth form v staff end of year games? Can you remember which side you cheered for? And, of course, the house games. Susan Moor had her head stood on during a netball match once. Not very refined young ladies when it came to competition!! The Good Work Marks and the four houses Rowan (red), Maple (yellow), Cedar (blue) and Linden (green). In the 2nd year they were changed to Ashley (yellow), Knight (red) and Gibbs (blue), all previous headmistresses, and they left out the green as they decided we were surrounded by the green grounds of the school. My sister remembers Miss Gibbs. Apparently, when she walked the corridors of the quadrangle, the groups of girls would part to allow her to walk up the middle. I think I remember seeing Miss Willis nearly flattened by a group of girls!! Not quite the same respect there!
Of course, if you're life has been too exciting then you do realise you'll make us all suicidal. I won't be able to attend the reunion, but I will be looking out for a photo of myself that can be scanned, emailed, enlarged to life size, printed and taken along so that I may be with you in spirit. I'm guessing it's still the sort of silly carry-on that you would be a party to, so keep an eye on your email.

Take care, and remember……….

Clowns to the left of me, jokers to the right……..here I am waiting for the next custard pie!! Anne XXX "

Andrea (Andie) Hodges joined the school when I think we were in the third year. She became a very good friend too. Andie lived with her nan and auntie because her mum was German and lived in Austria with her two sisters. She was one of the few people in our class whose parents were divorced. Her dad lived in Malaysia and was an airline engineer. In those days an engineer travelled on each flight. One summer holiday she went to stay with her dad. Whilst there she seemed to stop eating. After that she became obsessed with her weight and became thinner and thinner. She would eat but was throwing up in the toilet afterwards and took to manic skipping at lunchtime.

I think this picture was taken in the 4th or 5th form. We were standing in front of the science block.

Front Row – me, Caroline Bruce, Anne Schuster, Penny Charles

Hunched – Janice Tillyer

Back Row – Alison Bryant, Deena Clark, Andie Hodges

We were so concerned about Andie we went to see the headmistress (who by that time was Miss Kiff) and said that she had become "anorexic". Andie was furious with us. Ultimately she ended up in hospital – skeletal at 5 stone. Yet she was convinced she was fat. It really affected her mentally and she left the school moving down to the West Country and not telling us where she was going. It was all very sad and very odd. It was as though she blamed us for her anorexia, although the only comment I think I once made to her when she bemoaned the fact that she wanted to lose weight (before she became anorexic) was that perhaps she should cut out the 3 rounds of toast when she got home from school.

I have not heard from Andie since she left school quite suddenly in the 6th form and often wonder what became of her.

I could be a bit of a hot head once I'd had my cage rattled. In fact Sarah Morgan reminded me only recently how she'd been sarcastic about a story that I thought was incredibly funny but she didn't. However, rather than just saying "I didn't find that funny" she just went on at length about how her "sides were splitting it was so funny", "I'm convulsed with laughter", "that was the absoluteliest funniest thing I've ever heard" etc etc. This annoyed me immensely and I poured a can of drink over her head. I don't remember that at all, probably because it was not a best thing to do to a mate. However, Sarah did say she felt that she deserved it for being such a cow!

I also remember an incident in the changing rooms when Margaret accused me of hiding her gym things. Despite my protestations to the contrary, she was adamant. I must admit I literally saw red I was so cross. I was very close to giving Margaret a good slap but managed to restrain myself, which is just as well as we've been good friends for years.

I must say that despite generally enjoying school, maths was not my favourite subject. So much so, that for most of my secondary school life I was in the bottom set for maths (known as division 4 – bottom of the "maths league"). When we had our mock GCE O-level exams in January 1976 the results were "disheartening". For the first paper I only managed a very sad 19% and the second paper 37%! However, Mr Robinson, our maths teach was my saviour. He was a lovely man who joined the school I think only earlier that year. He left the navy to become a teacher and was so obviously nautical- with his bushy black beard and dead straight posture. He had very blue twinkling eyes and made maths fun with his jovial attitude. However, it was all a bit late in the day to redeem us from the pit of O-level failure, so he came up with the idea to change tack...well I did say he was nautical. He suggested that we change to CSE but we only had one term to cover the syllabus, which was completely different. As an incentive, he put up a prize each week (box of chocolates) for the person who had completed the most maths homework. Needless to say I liked that incentive, being a bit of a piglet and would do reams of work and was winning the prize every week, until he decided that I'd better give someone else a chance! It worked though, I completed all the work, found it much easier and got a Grade 1 CSE.

I think this was one of the last rounders matches of the 5th form and various people dressed up in clothes that were part of my mum and dad's fancy dress wardrobe. Caroline was wearing my favourite outfit - a tiger suit that mum had made out of an old mohair coat ! That outfit has had lots of outings and was worn along with other costumes by the Hogg Robinson staff in 1996 when we were raising money for Children in Need and stood outside Holborn Tube in the lunchtime rattling our collecting buckets.

POSTSCRIPT 2019

We were invited back to the school for HOG's centenary celebrations in 2006. It was a lovely day and there were quite a number of people from our year group. Five of us travelled together in my car from Kent. Anne Schuster (Humphreys), Sandra Green (Bromwich), Claire Howard

(Elliott) and Liz Malyon (Tredget).

Some of my mum's friends, also 'Old Girls' attended. I seem to remember seeing Gladys Thompson and Rene Dobbs.

We were surprised to see that the quadrangle was still as it was when we were pupils. Still as cold and draughty in the winter. I was convinced it would have been glassed in these days.

Liz, Anne & I featured in this article in the South London Press.

Memories are made of this

ANNIVERSARY: from left, Camille Buchanan, 15, Shandelle Samuel, 15 and Sumia Labid, 14. Right, old girls from the class of 1972

MAGNUS ANDERSSON/26489/7 & 28

NOSTALGIA was the order of the day when hundreds of former pupils returned to school to celebrate its centenary.

Harris Girls' Academy, formerly Waverley School for Girls, welcomed 300 former and current staff and students to show how far the school has come since it opened in 1906.

The oldest ex-pupil attending was Mary Skinner, who graduated in 1945. She cut the cake with the school's youngest student on the day Gabrielle Ofurhie, 13.

Assistant principal Lindsay Nash said students enjoyed hearing stories of what their predecessors got up to. She said: "In a few cases they were shocked by the naughtiness of these old girls."

Originally in Peckham, Harris Girls' Academy moved to its current site in Homestall Road, East Dulwich, in 1931. More than 900 students attend Harris Girls'.

There were 95 pupils on the roll when the school first opened its doors.

SOUTH LONDON PRESS 10/11/2006

Before Covid I was in contact with the current Head, Carrie Senior about a visit to the school. In fact another reunion is long overdue. Perhaps this will be the year!

Incidentally, Mary Butterworth, mentioned in the previous chapter taught art during my A level years and occasionally taught me.

I have also, tracked down Andie Hodges, who left the school as soon as she was discharged from Guys Hospital in London. Rather coincidentally she lives just five minutes' walk from step-daughter Christine's house. She has five children, and three grandchildren. We had a reunion at the wonderful art exhibition which Sarah Morgan (now Sarah Martin) organised for her late husband, Nick Martin. It was at the Menier Gallery in London.

If you'd like to look at Nick's art work :

www.nickmartin.com or for the exhibition: www.meniergallery.com

Latter-day HOGs, Sue Tombs, Sandra Green and Christina Joslin

THE JOY OF BOOTS

I'd applied to all the branches of W H Smiths within a 10-mile radius of our house. I didn't want to commute too far as I'd spent the previous five years becoming intimately acquainted with the rusty green, grinding trains of British Rail. The lingering odour of their Woodbine musty interiors remaining ingrained in my nostrils for days. My joyous 25-mile round trip journey to school was a daily endurance test involving a train to salubrious New Cross and then two buses. My sister had worked at M&S Marble Arch but I had no plans to follow in her immaculatey , high-heeled, footsteps.

I was rather hoping for a local Saturday job. I'd set my sights firmly on the aspiring writer's hallowed territory: W H Smith. My ideal working venue, surrounded by a plethora of stationery; alluring floral notepads, a rainbow assortment of pens, reams of virginal white paper. Oh and of course, not forgetting, the books. Row upon row of novels, standing ready for inspection, like privates on parade.

But alas, it was not to be.

Instead, my first and only Saturday job, was at Boots the chemists in Dartford. It was a huge disappointment. I had an awful pink overall, when pink really wasn't in any way trendy. In fact seriously uncool.

Not only that, by the end of the day it was always grimy and stained, where I'd been heaving dusty boxes from the stock room to stack the Spartan shelves. Or someone's Alberto Balsam shampoo would have leaked over the sales counter, in a murky swampy green puddle. My delightful overall invariably smothered in the glutinous stuff. I am, without doubt, the ultimate dirt magnet!

It was the most uninspiring job. My manager, Mrs Belsher, was a limping, stubble-chinned ogre, who seemed to take great delight in bullying the vulnerable. Namely us Saturday girls. We stood quivering in our sweaty pink overalls, definitely Boots' second-rate citizens. Easy targets for abuse.

The highlight of the day would be lunchtime when my sister, five years my senior, would appear at the till, asking me to put aside some item of No 7 to purchase later when I could get my staff discount.

Then she would whisk me away to her enchanted regions of the boutiques and shoe shops. She was by then working as a PA in Chancery Lane. She had a very well paid job and spent most of her money on fashion items. My best friend Lesley and I were in awe of her style and glamour. I didn't have the same dedication to fashion, but I did take some interest in what she was buying. I knew that when she was bored with that bee-like tank top or the oh-so-cutesy Laura Ashley dress, it would come my way. A poignant memory rises from the ancient mists. The vision transports me back to a boutique in Dartford, watching her strut around in her black platform boots and swirling a purple midi coat, like a top model on a catwalk, her auburn hair fanning out behind. A haunting melody as backdrop to this scene: The Moody Blues' 'Nights in White Satin'. I only have to hear that tune and I think of that particular incident. I also remember picturing myself in that coat in six months' time but somehow couldn't see me wearing it with the same panache. Certainly not with platform boots!

My proper job was some years later, after I'd spent ten months in Austria sort of working for Silver Lodge Holidays. Although in reality, it was really more like an extended holiday. In the winter months an alpine wonderland of glittering sun on snow. In summer months, a symphony of tinkling of cowbells, or the old-fashioned steam produced 'toot, toot' of the Ziller Valley train. Then you would open the red gingham curtains to a scene identical to 'The Sound of Music'. I was always disappointed not to see Julie Andrews as Maria cavorting down the mountainside. Was this a real job? Definitely not. It was an idyll. No real job would allow its staff to spend every afternoon during the months of February to April skiing, kamikaze-like, through some of the most breath-taking scenery in Austria. There I met Laura Turley, whose parents owned one of the chalets. When Silver Lodge's Austrian operation closed down, I accompanied Laura back to the UK via the 'Romantische Strasse', the most scenic route back through Germany.

Settling into a proper adult, sensible job didn't come until I was twenty-three.

I went for an interview at Deutsches Reisebuero (DER Travel) after trawling the papers for suitable travel related jobs. On the strength of my knowledge of Austria and Germany's Romantisch Strasse, together with my get-by-in-German, the job was offered on the spot. DER in Orchard Street, London, just opposite Selfridges became a very formative experience. I quickly took on some serious adult responsibilities.

My boss Hans Woerndl, although a tyrant and a difficult man to please, gave me my first step on the corporate travel ladder. When one of my colleagues in the Business Travel Department, announced her imminent new arrival, Herr Woerndl summoned me to the hallowed space of his office. We were always anxious at such a request. Normally a serious chastisement for some unfortunate error. I shuffled in awaiting my fate. Yet instead of a reprimand, he offered me a transfer to the prestigious Business Travel Department. Rather taken aback, I stuttered:

'But I know nothing about business travel'

His retort was:

'No, but you vill learn'.

It was a very steep learning curve. Sometimes I felt I was back in Fuegen again, climbing some treacherous pinnacle. Nevertheless, I was very grateful for the opportunity. In less than 2 years, I had attended numerous British Airways' ticketing courses after work and became the supervisor of the department.

Our major client was the prestigious Mercedes Benz. My best experience with this client, was escorting some prize-winners to USA and Mexico.

The top ten sales men at Mercedes had won this rather wonderful 'incentive prize'. I couldn't believe my luck when Hans asked if I would escort the group from Dallas to Mexico. Mercedes Benz's Managing Director, Hans Tauscher normally escorted these incentive trips. However, he had other commitments and could only take the salesmen and their accompanying wives, as far as New York. What a responsibility. It was the first time I'd flown on business, let alone business class. I had to meet the group in Dallas, take them round to see the sights there, including the Southfork ranch of 'Dallas' fame.

Then after a few days there, it was off to the five star, ultra-chic Pierre Marques Hotel in Acapulco, Mexico. It was a joy rather than a chore to look after this delightful group. They were all lovely couples who didn't want me fussing over them. In fact, they wanted to look after me. Most of them had kids my age.

For another trip, I had to charter a plane for 23 people to Seville, Spain. It was for a new car test drive. The only thing available was a Boeing 707 with over a hundred seats, so I asked the airline to remove quite a lot of the seats, to allow the guests to 'stretch out and relax'. I had to accompany them to ensure my meticulous arrangements went to plan, including all the Mercedes branded headrests, napkins and crockery. The catering was oh so special too, the like of which you do not see on normal services. Posh canapés, lobster, champagne corks popping by the dozen. It was quite a party.

I sat next to the presenter of Top Gear. Certainly not Jeremy Clarkson. Tom Coyne, a grey-haired guy in his fifties. It was long before the programme had acquired such a cult following. The trip was short but intensely sweet, with many other trips to follow over the years. It was definitely the start of my lifelong love affair with travel.

A far cry from that Saturday job at Boots.

No boots but sandals!

My role model and lovely sister, Gillian.

Sadly no longer with us.

THE JOYFUL CANTERBURY TALES

In October 1977 my suitcases and portable typewriter were all packed in to Martin Venier's Austin 1100 to take me to my digs in South Street, Canterbury. Because I had gone through the clearing system, all the spaces for living in the University were taken. Not that there were many in the first place at Kent University. It probably would have been easier had Mum and Dad dropped me off as it was very difficult saying goodbye to Martin, particularly as he had not done well in his A-levels and was going to have to re-take them in order to go on to University. He originally wanted to study dentistry but because he was not very good when it came to the exams, he had decided on Geology.

It was sad that the enforced separation coupled with the distractions of university life meant that the relationship petered out before the end of the first year.

It wasn't an easy transition from home to university, particularly as I was not 'living in'. In 'Fresher's Week' it was an endless round of social activities and parties. Not having a base in the college I did feel somewhat left out. Everyone seemed to be finding friends – normally people living in their same blocks. By the end of the first week, I was not happy. I had been walking home from the university to my digs – an hour's walk when the buses had stopped running. During that first week I rang my mum and cried

' I hate it here and I won't be staying. I'm miles away from the University and feel like an outsider. It's awful. I'll see you at the weekend'.

Mum told me not to be so hasty but to come home at the weekend and we'll think of a solution to the problem.

The solution came in the form of a second hand bike (£60) which I personalised. I called it the 'Stow Flyer' and proudly hand painted its name on the plate above the chain. I'd always wanted a bike and it had taken 18 years to get one.

I do have to say though, that my trusty steed did once get me in to trouble. One night when I'd had more than a few pints of cider (yes cider…) and cycled down Tyler Hill back to South Street. The hill is very steep and at one point curves. Unfortunately the road curved and I didn't and consequently my 'Stow Flyer' jettisoned me into the pillar of one the houses on the bend! Not surprisingly I saw stars and may possibly have been unconscious for a few moments. I guess the cider and shock anaesthetised me as I wasn't in pain.

I had a basket on the front of the 'Stow Flyer' and the contents were spilled across the gravel driveway. I picked up what I could see by moonlight, climbed back on to my fortunately, undamaged bike and continued on my way. I got back to the house, went to get my keys from my bag only to find they were missing. I had to cycle back to the accident scene to scrabble around in the gravel and eventually found my keys which had been propelled into the bushes. Oh dear! It seemed like a very long journey home.

It was only the next morning when I ventured out of my very small room to go to the bathroom, when I met my landlady, Frieda, who shrieked in horror 'What have you done to your face?'. I went to the bathroom, looked in the mirror to find that I had an enormous bloodied graze on the side of my face where I had hit the pillar. Later in the day not only did I have a hangover but I also started to feel the effects of my contretemps with brick work. Not only that, but over subsequent days I found that I was missing all sorts of small items – lipstick, pen, etc and had to stop on numerous occasions looking under bushes for my belongings. Luckily the owners of the house didn't catch me rooting around in their garden, on all fours with only my bum showing in their bushes.

I spent of the rest of the year living in South Street with Freda, Eddie and their kids and the rabbit. They were a really nice family. Although I kept in touch with them for a while, I don't know if they are still there or have moved.

Needless to say, that with the aid of my bike, I did settle in to University. I did also make some friends, which helped – Shireen Agnew, Hilary Walker, the two Bernadettes – Bernie and Barnie and also some of the 2nd and 3rd year students – Kieran Hearty and Dirimo Ocando to name but a few. In my second year I became friendly with Carolyn Clews and Ruth Collyer, who were in their first year.

I also got involved in the badminton club and joined the editorial team of the University newspaper – 'Incant'. Sounds quite grand but it was not really, as I was the Features Editor, the job no one else wanted! This meant I had to find all the filler bits for the paper. Funny stories, crosswords etc. I also covered a few of the concerts for the Features section, which meant I saw the gigs for free. I also took the photos as I had a decent SLR Nikon, courtesy of Dad who had upgraded to a better camera. I enjoyed attending the emerging band concerts. Tom Robinson Band was one who had just had a hit with the unforgettable '2,4,6,8 Motorway'. Also Dexy's Midnight Runners (of 'C'mon Eileen' fame), and Manhattan Transfer ('Chanson d'Amour'). I did however, do a few stints as roving reporter on some 'serious' stories and covered 'NUPE's day of Action' when all the University's support staff went on strike. This meant that the canteens, serveries and bars were closed for the day. Shock! Horror! No food, no drink! The cleaners were also on strike but as you can imagine that didn't bother the students at all.

There is so much more I could expand on but I'll leave it until I write the book. But suffice to say I still am in contact with Carolyn and Ruth. Less frequently, Kieran Hearty and Hilary Walker. Kieran is known for organising a good party. I met my ex Graham at one almost 40 years ago! Kieran arranged two fabulous parties for his 60th and 65th. Excelling as a stand up comedian. His retirement 'job'. He was always a bit of a comic at UKC!

If you would like to see Kieran in action, look at this Youtube clip:

https://www.youtube.com/watch?v=jTi3DU9s2dM&t=28s

The Joy of Music

YOU ONLY LIVE TWICE

One of our writing exercises for our Medway Mermaids' group was to choose a piece of evocative music.

My choice was 'You Only Live Twice' from the James Bond theme tunes.

That piece of music transports me back to the lounge in my first Victorian home in Camberwell, London. On wintry evenings in that spacious but chilly high ceilinged room, we would huddle round our two bar electric fire. My sister and I would study the imitation coal and flickering pretend flame, whilst my dad set up 'The Holiday Slide Show'. He was a keen photographer, always taking hundreds of slides wherever we went.

He would ceremoniously bring out the ironing board, where he carefully placed the slide projector. Then he would precariously wobble on the red and grey settee, trying to attach the large white screen to the permanent hook above the shiny beige and brown ceramic fireplace. With the precision of a maestro, he would delicately place the reel-to- reel tape on the Siemens tape recorder, with his pre-recorded 'holiday music'.

The first time he used this music, was after our first trip abroad. Spain. It all seemed wildly exotic, glamorous and very foreign at the time. We would dim the lights, start the music, then let the automated slide projector weave its magic. There was a whole host of tunes to accompany our holiday slides. 'Born free' was also another favourite. However, it was 'You Only Live Twice' that for me, held a special key to unlocking those precious holiday memories. I well up when I hear it. I identify it so closely, not only with those wonderful holidays but also with my very special, funny, musical, artistic Dad.

It whisked us back to the sandy beaches and warm water of the Med or the pine-clad hills surrounding the resort. You could practically smell the fresh tang of pine. I sometimes wondered whether Dad had sneakily given a blast of the air freshener. Whatever his tricks of the trade, like a consummate magician he conjured a magnificent magical hour or two, warming up an otherwise cold winter's evening.

THE JOY OF SAX

Sunday 19 February 2012.

My surprise Christmas present was finally unveiled – but only once we'd reached Kensington.

'Are we going to the Royal Albert Hall?' I asked, excitement and anticipation in equal measure, once we had passed the familiar imposing shop front of 'Harrods'.

We parked our rather mundane (and not too clean) Zafira on one of those really smart, leafy squares within walking distance of the Royal Albert Hall. Two Community Support Officers immediately accosted us on bikes. Oh dear had we parked where we shouldn't or perhaps we looked like potential burglars? Panic over. No they just wanted us to pose with them for the Police Intranet. Who knows, we may now be faces of Joe and Missus Public in police circles?

Ralph, always the tease, wouldn't tell me what we were going to see. Revelation time. The first floor eatery at the Royal Albert Hall was our destination. The Ignite restaurant is light, airy, very cool and contemporary. A statement piece of artwork is suspended from the ceiling on flimsy wires; huge mirrors, reminiscent of something us ladies would use for magnifying those irritating stray facial hairs. Not sure how the cleaners cope with such a display. Huge canvasses of famous rock artists adorn the walls. Just behind Ralph's head was the craggy face of Paul Weller. We always have problems remembering that particular artist but after him looming over us for 3 hours, we will never forget his name.

We were at one of the 'Ignite Brunch' sessions where they have a group playing through the brunch service. This session features the Darius Brubeck Jazz Quartet. Although I am not an aficionado, I do love some occasional jazz and particularly a bit of sax. Immediately I knew who Darius was. The Dave Brubeck Quartet shot to fame in the 60's with their rendition of 'Take Five'. Ironically, Dave is a jazz pianist and not saxophonist. Yet the saxophone solo is synonymous with that piece. Darius follows in his father's fingertips by also being a jazz pianist. Darius told us that Dave was still enjoying Jazz but no longer touring at the grand age of 92. Sadly, later on in the year we had heard that Dave passed away.

We enjoyed a jazz odyssey whilst happily munching through our eggs, bacon and endless cups of tea. The music was great, the breakfast service less so. I had to remind the waiter 3 times for my pot of tea but that was the only criticism of our 'Ignite Brunch'. The strains of the piano, double bass, guitar and particularly the Sax, resonated around the lofty restaurant. Quavers, crochets and minims positively bounced off the walls and the vibrating tones hit a chord deep within my core. Darius on the piano was brilliant. His nimble fingers ran up and down the key board, with such skill and dexterity. However, for me the sax hits the right spot. Those trilling, thrilling, sometimes discordant highs and then the deep vibrating sexy low notes that send my heart into frenzy. Dave O'Higgins is a master of this amazing instrument and made me yearn to play. Despite a musical family, I only could play the humble recorder.

'Ralph' I caught my husband's rapt attention 'It's no good....I MUST learn the sax'.

'Oh no' my long suffering husband grimaced 'not another hobby...you physically don't have the time!'

'I must make the time,' I mouthed, resolutely.

Whilst Dave O'Higgins was packing away his saxophone, I felt compelled to speak to him (much to my husband's dismay).

'That was really inspirational. I'm wondering if it's not too late to learn the sax. I have been thinking about it for the last few years'

'Thank you' he graciously replied and then added, 'do you play any musical instrument?'

'Only the recorder' I sheepishly admitted. 'And I did have a go on my niece's saxophone a few years ago'

'Well, the recorder's a really good start as the basic fingering is the same'. Dave advised, adding, 'Besides that, it's never too late if you're keen'

'Right then' I said having made my mind up. 'I shall investigate lessons next week. Thank you so, so much.'

'Marvellous' Dave enthusiastically replied, 'I'm sure you won't regret it...and best of luck with the lessons!'

I skipped back to Ralph patiently waiting at the table. He raised his eyebrow, enquiringly.

'Well then, what did he say?' he asked.

'That it's a good start that I can play the recorder and it's never too late to learn.'

'Wrong answer!' said Ralph jokingly.

We made our way back to the car. I was inwardly skipping. It was as if all my Christmases had come at once, I was so excited.

The next morning, my friend Jackie came to visit. She lives in Chessington, so we don't often get together. However, this particular day I said I was treating her to lunch in Rochester (this time courtesy of Mr Tesco). Fate must have definitely been guiding us, as after the obligatory tour of all the shops, our last port of call was the Oxfam shop. No sooner had we stepped through the door, Jackie noticed a music stand with a sheet announcing:

'Saxophone and clarinet lessons. First lesson's fee will be donated to Oxfam. For further details contact Dave.'

This was definitely an OMG moment and I immediately went to the counter and asked about the teacher.

'Oh Dave's a lovely guy' said the friendly assistant 'He volunteers one morning a week. Would you like me to write down his number?'

'YES PLEASE' I said without a moment's hesitation.

I left the shop clutching my precious post it note. As soon as Jackie left I was dialling Dave's number and arranging my first lesson. Swiftly I had to find a saxophone. Luckily, my niece Holly still has hers. She hasn't played for some time. She said I could borrow it to see how I got on.

Now, on 3rd July 2013, I am eighteen months into my personal musical odyssey. It isn't the easiest of journeys. At times, it is positively an uncomfortable and frustrating one. It accentuates my short-term memory issues. I often look at a piece of music and have forgotten the relation of notes to the gleaming brass buttons. The mouthpiece has crinkled my lips and my less than nimble fingers ache from the effort.

For all of those tribulations it is something that has brought a new dimension to my life and by default, my husband's.

We've been to various Jazz gigs...even as far as Brussels last year. However, on our doorstep, Medway seems to be teaming with jazz and sax opportunities. We've enjoyed the Eagle Tavern in Rochester, The Hastings Arms in Gillingham (Dave, my tutor, runs the Rochester Swing Preservation Society). In June, we sampled the jazz delights at the Brooke Theatre - King Pleasure and the Biscuit Boys. They were fun, boisterous and seemed to have an entourage of jiving dancers. Last night, again at the Brooke, the award winning Derek Nash Acoustic Quartet were the stars. Derek played every type of sax...soprano, alto, tenor and baritone with such verve, energy and conviction. He bucked and hopped all over the stage, constantly smiling; the happiest man in the world. Fantastic. His Pianist Dave Newton, has won best jazz pianist at the British Jazz Awards for 10 years running. What a virtuoso. It was a sublime evening's entertainment. Even if the theatre is looking a bit worse for wear with its peeling interior façade and damp-damaged curtains.

The sax, without doubt is a truly wonderful instrument. It invigorates if you are feeling lethargic; a low mood transformed in a breath to a high. It can also be quite emotional. There are certain pieces that are strongly associated with my dead parents. 'Largo from Dvorak's New World Symphony' reminds me of my dad, sitting between his huge (homemade) loudspeakers conducting his imaginary orchestra in perfect stereo.

'Girl from Ipanema' was my mum's signature Hammond organ piece. When playing these beautiful melodies my parents' presence is palpable. My nose prickles with the inevitable tears flowing as I sense their hazy outlines, nodding in approval. I am not so sure my neighbours are nodding their heads the same way, possibly shaking them in dismay.

Oh and I need my own saxophone.

I am definitely hooked.

Last night we were told about a very special sax auction on Ebay currently. The Johnny Hodges Vito/LeBlanc alto saxophone complete with a diamond-eyed snakehead as the octave key. Although my husband has promised to buy me a saxophone, I don't think he'll be putting in a bid. The reserve is USD 150,000. Derek Nash told us that he was hoping for a lottery win to put in a bid.

But you really don't have to be a millionaire to enjoy this instrument.

Thank you Adolph Sax.

Postscript – 15 July 2013

On one of the best summer days so far this year, we should have been heading off to the coast to dip our toes in the cooling sea.

Instead, we were venturing in to the impressive Sax & Co unit on an industrial estate in Crowborough. In the sweltering heat of one of their sound proofed booths, I tested out a selection of their instruments. The prices ranged from £399- £844. I put the four instruments through their paces with the pieces I can play without the music – 'summertime', 'Moon River', & 'Greensleeves'. It wasn't the easiest of tasks....my fingers were slippery with sweat and kept slipping off the keys. In fact, the beads of perspiration were oozing out of every pore as concentration and heat got the better of me. I played the instruments again a second time to give them the benefit of the doubt. Not surprisingly, the most expensive instrument came out tops. I am now the proud owner of a glistening golden brand new Yamaha.

It is without doubt the most prized present I have ever received and I will treasure it. I am sure there will come a time when my fingers will cease up and my lungs will not have the power and my slack, withered lips unable to produce a note. When that happens, I shall then have it sitting in the corner on its stand, dusting it, cherishing it and proclaiming its beauty for all to behold.

THE JOY OF CUXTONES

Wednesday evening in 'term time' is now pure delight.

Singing with the CuxTones.

The CuxTones Community Choir was in my consciousness for a couple of years but I'd never had the opportunity to hear them sing, or participate.

Working from home changed that.

I initially went to CuxTones in the summer of 2016 to discuss with Sarah, the choir leader and singing teacher, some lessons for Ralph. He thoroughly enjoys singing but fails to sing in tune.

I knew I would become a CuxTone that very first evening as they were practising a medley from my favourite musical – 'Lion King.' It was a definite example of serendipidty.

Listening and then joining in with the harmonious voices of this small choir, was such an incredibly moving moment. The tears welled up and my nose painfully prickled after the first few chords. 'Lion King' does that to me. I've seen 'Lion King' three times and for most of the performance I am bawling!

So inevitably, by the end of the song, Julia was offering me a much neded tissue.

Since then I have participated in two summer and three Christmas concerts. We have even performed at Bluewater's Christmas festivities three years running.

I've been introduced to numerous songs that I didn't know. 'A Thousand Years' is another tear-jerker which has me reaching for those Handy Andys.

Our choir leader, Sarah, creates some fantastic three part arrangements. During the day she teaches, mainly musical theatre. Then she also undertakes occasional evening gigs with the Barbara Streisand songbook. She does a great Barbara!

Go to Sarah Starkey School of Singing Facebook page for a listen.

One of the Cuxtones' Christmas parties. Pre Covid!

Postscript 2022

Sadly since Covid 19 turned the whole world upside-down, CuxTones merged with the Meopham Choir and morphed into Village Voices.

THE JOY OF SKYLARKS

Another singing opportunity presented itself when I attended a dementia awareness event one Friday back in 2016. I had the fortune to hear Dr Trish Vella-Burrows talking about her therapeutic work with music and more specifically, with her research and involvement with Medway Skylarks.

The next day I turned up with MIL (Mother-in-Law) Olive at St Mary's Island Community Centre only to find an empty hall. Ringing Trish's number I learnt they were performing in Hoo that day, a detail which had not been shared the previous day. Unabashed, the following week we joined the group for their singing and co-ordinational exercises. A more joyful group you could not wish to meet.

Two years on we are still a part of this group. Martin Nagler seems to have taken over stewardship of Medway Skylarks and it is growing from strength to strength, with various invitations to play at AGMs, Christmas Fairs, Christmas lighting up ceremonies and anywhere that would like to hear this wonderful group.

Thank you Medway Skylarks and in particular, Trish, Nicola Vella, Ben, Martin, Phil Bungay, Dr John Cornwall, Phil Self, and not forgetting our lovely tea and coffee provider, Maggi.

During the Covid period, Sue Lovell held many of the Skylarks together leading the singing through Zoom.

For more information regarding Medway Skylarks and the Medway Neurological Network please visit:
http://medwayneuro.org.uk/index.php?p=1_14

Also enjoy the marvellous Isolation Choir, led by Phil Self.

One of the great opportunities to come out of the awful pandemic:

'Wild Mountain Thyme'
https://www.youtube.com/watch?v=uOlSklHoL7g

'What a wonderful World'
https://www.youtube.com/watch?v=ZARDxLv4zVo

and not least, the rather eery but beautiful 'Drones'. No doubt inspired by 'drone master' Brian Eno who can be seen singing on 'What a Wonderful World'.

https://www.youtube.com/watch?v=AQkPgU_BUXo

(I played my saxophone on this one!)

POSTSCRIPT FEBRUARY 2022

Through my continuing participation with Skylarks, we had the opportunity to sing at the Non Visible Disability Initiative in September 2021. It was in Rochester Cathedral. Only the second 'live' event for Skylarks since Covid 19.

The Key Note Speaker was Professor David Wilkinson, explaining about his ground-breaking work with Parkinson's Disease. He is championing the world's first integrated Parkinson's Disease Centre at my old alma mater, the University of Kent. I have supported UKC over the years, attending their Careers Fairs as an employer and then as a minor benefactor. This project caught our attention as Parkinson's is the fastest growing neurological condition worldwide. I am sure integrated research will benefit all neurological conditions. We have a number of close family friends affected by PD. We are now volunteer fundraisers. For further details visit:
https://www.kent.ac.uk/parkinsons

World Parkinson's Day at Hempstead Valley 11 April 2018

THE JOY OF SNAPE MALTINGS – AN EPIPHANY?

27-28 January 2020

At our Skylarks' group on Saturday 25 January, Dr Trish Burrows, our facilitator that day, mentioned this course at Snape Maltings starting on the Monday :

https://snapemaltings.co.uk/project/sing-to-beat-parkinsons-practitioner-training/

Despite the late notice, I decided that I could easily rearrange my appointments for those two days. Having established that there was no one I could travel with, I set out at 3pm on the Sunday. I really didn't want to contend with the Dartford Crossing in the early hours to get to Suffolk for a 09.30 start. It was dry when I set out but only 2 miles along the A228 it started to drizzle. The drizzle then became a persistent downpour, accompanied by the tedious screech of windscreen wipers. Two hours into the very slow journey, it was dark as well as very wet. The gleam of headlights reflecting off the sodden roads, along with the spray form other cars' tyres made driving unpleasant. Just coming off a roundabout near Coggleshall, I misread the road in the glistening darkness and hit the kerb with an unnerving 'thwack'. The tyre immediately burst, bringing my poor little car to a bumpy halt.

'Oh Eff' I wailed.

It was a busy dual carriageway. Not the best place to have a flat and I certainly was not going to change the tyre. Rifling through my purse for an RAC card, which didn't exist, I then looked through the glove box. In my panic I couldn't find the membership confirmation letter which was there. A case of negative hallucination. So it was the inevitable call to Ralph:

'You never guess what? I've had a tyre blow out. I can't find the membership number for the RAC. Do you have it handy?'

Ralph disappeared for what seemed an eternity. It obviously wasn't handy. Ever optimistic he commented:

'Oh you've probably ruined the tracking if you hit the kerb that hard. The car won't be drivable. The car will have to be towed home and I will then have to take you to Snape Maltings. I bet it will be hours before the RAC get to you.'

Despite his gloomy prediction, the very sodden RAC guy, Anthony, was with me within half an hour, changed the tyre very efficiently despite the heavy rain. I was sheltering under a bus shelter, by the pull-in where I'd managed to park the car waiting for the RAC. I was at least dry, unlike poor Anthony, who hadn't been dry all afternoon. I felt obliged to give him a £5.00 tip. I'd probably been one of a number of dizzy blonde women bursting tyres in the wet conditions. Also the tracking was fine. I continued on my way without the assistance of a tow truck. However, what should have been a journey of just over two hours was four and a half hours. Not helped by a rather wayward satnav that took me down some very narrow B roads. Weary, I found The Crown Inn, Snape, where I'd booked for the two nights. I made my dramatic stumbling entrance trying to carry overnight bags, saxophone case and handbag. In the process dropping my purse, scattering money and cards in all directions. Teresa, the landlady came to my rescue.

Despite taking my saxophone, I never had the opportunity to play it in the auditorium. Not only that, I was so in the clouds after the course, I actually left my saxophone on a seat in the auditorium. Luckily, Trish picked it up and took it home with her to Deal then brought it back to St Mary's Island for our Skylarks' session. It had quite a round trip and had a few days' stay at the seaside. It would have been a very long drive if I had to return to collect my prized possession from Snape Maltings. I am sooooo blonde.

It's difficult to put in to words the experience. It was one you need participate in. Hopefully some of the content will be on the Canterbury Cantata Trust website in due course. The whole two days was professionally filmed.

Snape Maltings is an eclectic collection of buildings which have been renovated and transformed into various music auditoriums and practice rooms. It also has a fantastic shop, café and pub. It's a scenic location, adjacent to the river in Aldeburgh, Suffolk. It was originally where they delivered the barley to turn into malt. Snape is well known by music aficionados. The Aldeburgh Music Festival, established by Benjamin Britten, is held there each year.

The final chapter in this saga happened this week. I opened an official looking letter from the Essex Police. I had been speeding in a 40 mph zone. Oh dear, it had become a very expensive course, what with the £73.00 for a new tyre and probably £60.00 fine.

Still I wouldn't change a thing. I am now an authorised practitioner of the 'Sing to Beat Parkinsons' programme. I am now intending to set up Skylark group in Cuxton School and maybe a group at Gravesham Community Hospital, where my daughter, Amelia, is a Speech & Language Therapist.

It's been somewhat of an epiphany. I've always loved singing and music, but perhaps I've finally found my vocation. It's just taken a very long time.

Perhaps a new career after early retirement?

POST SCRIPT FEBRUARY 2022

I've had a return trip to Snape Maltings. But this time with Ralph and Cara Vann, the third 'person' in our relationship. We stayed at a lovely CL Caravan and Motorhome Club Site. Thoroughly recommended. Run by farmer, John Bater https://www.caravanclub.co.uk/certificated-locations/england/suffolk/framlingham/church-farm-1/

The great thing about this location, apart from it's peaceful beauty, was it's proximity to Snape Maltings. Ralph had established as part of the Aldeburgh Music Festival, there were free outdoor concerts during July and August. We had three lovely, if blowy, concerts. In fact, the third performance by the amazing duet, Avawaves, the rather oppressive, windy weather adding ambience to their amazing opening number. I cried.

https://brittenpearsarts.org/visit-us/snape-maltings

THE JOY OF THE LITERARY WORLD

THE JOY OF MERMAIDS

Written for 'Mermaid Tails'

published November 2016

I feel privileged to be a member of a very special group.

In 2011, I discovered Medway Mermaids.

Despite the evocative title, we are not as you might think, a swimming group. Although, much to our chagrin, we have recently discovered there is a synchronized swimming group in Gravesend by the same name. No, we are a women's writing group. I guess we do swim, but only metaphorically!

What I love about my fellow Mermaids is their boundless enthusiasm and a prevailing attitude of 'if I can do it, you can do it'. I always believed writing to be a pretty solitary occupation but since joining this group, I never feel alone when I am writing. Invariably only an e-mail away, one of our members is quick to respond to a query. A more helpful bunch of individuals would be difficult to find.

Each month we exchange our lovingly crafted pieces and await the response. The tension mounts whilst waiting for the feedback; there are always numerous critiques. After the suggested edits it builds confidence to submit our pieces elsewhere.

I still have a way to go before I join the ranks of properly published Mermaids. Susan Pope, Lin Tidy, and June Winton have all been conscientious in finishing and publishing novels.

However, it is Elizabeth Haynes who has achieved both commercial and critical acclaim with her psychological thrillers 'Into the Darkest Corner', Revenge of the Tide', 'Human Remains' and 'Under a Silent Moon'. In fact she was Amazon's Star of 2011 for the first of these books.

Whether published or not, we all appreciate everyone's efforts, are totally inclusive and share in every individual's successes or inevitably, the occasional disappointment.

I can't bear the thought of having to jump through the numerous tedious hoops of traditional publishing. Now there are excellent opportunities provided with e-books or low cost self-publishing. Lin Tidy discovered the first-rate Arts Council funded FeedaRead after a disappointing setback with her original publisher. I now see that there will be a whole Mermaid family of books gracing the FeedaRead website, after we have swum together and created our own literary waves. Each one of us with our own Mermaid tale……

Mermaids performing at the Rochester Lit Fest

Eastgate House June 2018

THE JOY OF AUTHORS
An Afternoon with Jill Murphy
July 2018

Back in 2003, when I was working for the Medway Dyslexia Association, I came across an application for funding by The Millennium Reading Awards. It was to engage individuals in community projects. It was too good an opportunity to pass up, so I put in an application for my project, 'Books R Kool 4 All'.

Several months later, I was delighted to learn I had received an award of £3,500. I duly went to the presentation ceremony in London. The Mayor of Camden presented the winners with their awards. I then set to work putting everything in place for the six-month project. It was a success, with four events attended by more than 300 children and adults.

The most exciting spin off from this project, was reuniting my friend Jackie Dixon, with one of the carers from the children's home she lived in until she was eleven years old. Jackie had created a lovely book on nail art and had agreed to be a volunteer doing nail art with the attendees. I had been busily writing to high profile authors to see if I could get any of them to come to Medway to inspire with tales of how they became authors. JK Rowling was top of the list but Jackie said:

'Why don't you try Jill Murphy? I knew her when I was in the children's home.'

'Really? I love Jill Murphy's books. We have known each other more than twenty-five years, Jackie and you have never told me this before. Was she in care?'

'No, she was one of the care assistants. She was my favourite. Even back then, she was writing. She created an illustrated story book for every child in the home in Surbiton. Or in my case...children. She wrote a story for my brother Andrew and me.'

'That's amazing Jackie. Do you have a copy of the book?'

'No, sadly not, but I do have a signed copy of the first edition of the

'The Worst Witch'. Jill sent it to me at the children's home, although by then Andrew and I had been adopted, so it was sent on to our new home.'

'Have you never tried to get in contact with her?' I asked.

'No. She's too famous now and I doubt she would remember me after all these years.'

Jill Murphy, in case you do not know, is very well known for her 'Worst Witch' stories and her delightful toddler books. My kids loved the captivating Large family in 'Five Minutes Peace' & 'A Piece of Cake'. So much so, that I can repeat the whole of 'Five Minutes Peace' without even opening the book. Without further ado, I wrote to Jill Murphy on Medway Dyslexia Association headed paper inviting her to come along to one of the 'Books R Kool 4 All' roadshows. I thought it would be a fantastic surprise for Jackie if she were able to attend one of the events. Jackie had committed to come to every event, even though it involved a round trip journey of 75 miles from Chessington.

I thought I might catch Jill Murphy's attention by sending her a copy of my book 'Georgia's Fantastic Christmas'. Georgia, my Goddaughter is Jackie's only child. I wrote the book for her as a special present, I also thought it might be a good fund-raiser for the Cystic Fibrosis Trust. Georgia suffers from that life limiting condition. I explained this in my covering letter.

Ralph, during his lunch break, duly dropped the letter and book into Puffin Publishers in the Strand. That was on Wednesday. On Friday, I received a phone call at work from Jill Murphy. I was gobsmacked. She was delighted that I had sent her the letter and book, asking if she could have Jackie's phone number.

'But I haven't even told her yet' I admitted. She gave me her number to pass on to Jackie. Sadly, as she lives in Cornwall it was rather difficult for her to attend any of the events but she promised to 'send something in the post'

Jackie and Jill subsequently had a very long chat over the phone and promised to meet up.

A week or so later, a huge box turned up at the MDA offices. I opened it expecting it to be boring stationery. No, it was practically the whole collection of Jill's books, all beautifully signed with her distinctive calligraphic 'Love from' and then signature. Overwhelmed by her kind generosity, I phoned to thank her. We were on the phone for over an hour. I found that our lives and interests were very similar. She obviously loves books and art, as do I. She also has as dyslexic son, the same age as my son Greg. Amelia, my daughter is dyslexic.

Jill also lived in Chessington in her early life. I had previously lived in Chessington. She also said she would try to come to Medway to do an event for the Medway Dyslexia Association. I was hoping to arrange something along the lines of 'An Audience with Jill Murphy'. Consequently, we had an ongoing correspondence and phone calls over the years but never got to meet. She did however go to see Jackie when she was in London, some years after I had reunited them. As it happened, Amelia, my daughter, happened to be at Jackie's at the time and was delighted to meet Jill and chat books with her. Georgia, sadly did not have the same interest in books, so whilst Jackie made tea, my daughter had Jill's undivided attention. I was very envious when Amelia rang me later to tell me.

In 2015 Medway Mermaids launched 'Mermaid Tails' I invited Jill but again her schedule didn't allow it. I sent her a copy instead. At the same time, I asked if she might do some illustrated bookplates for James, our grandson.

Several years earlier, she had done some for Sophie, our granddaughter. On her Christmas card that year, she added a note:

Dear Judith

Thanx for your lovely card and all your news. I ***loved*** *the anthology and have read half of it already. It is really good – such a lot of talented people.*

I am not well at the moment – lots of trips to hosp in London and will probably be out of action for Jan and Feb. Trying madly to finish W. Witch no 8 so won't have time to take on anything extra. Have enclosed cheque for £30 to cover the £20 you sent me plus £10 for the anthology which didn't have a price, do hope 2016 is good for you and yours.

Love from Jill x

In fact, the treatment, which was for a return of breast cancer, took much longer than January and February, lasting a year and a half.

This summer, we decided to have a short respite break in Babbacombe, Devon. I ascertained that it was only 90 minutes' drive from Jill's house in Cornwall. We had driven very close to her village when we went to Cornwall a couple of years ago but I did not like to just 'pop in'. Ralph was not against the idea of a 90-minute drive. Given that some of our commutes to London were longer than that, it would be a pleasant diversion in comparison. I sent another e-mail to Jill, checking if she was OK and advising of our imminent trip. Our plan was to take her out to lunch...maybe Rick Stein's in Padstow. She suggested we went to her house for lunch instead.

We could not turn up empty handed. I decided some plant arrangements in pots would be a well-received gift.

However, there were no suitable pre-planted pots, so had to ask the nursery if they would pot them, if we selected the plants. They were extremely helpful. In the meantime, we went for a coffee in their rather steamy café. There had been a tremendous deluge of rain, which after the long dry spell was creating an intensely humid atmosphere. Not unlike Singapore. Truly tropical Cornwall!

We loaded the pots carefully in the car but I still was not very happy with the display.

'Could we perhaps pop into the nursery near where Jill lives and see if they have any trailing plants. I'm sure that's what they need.'

Ralph, ever accommodating, although after a bit of eye rolling, agreed. We found some suitable additional plants at our next stop. We of course had to rearrange the plants in the nursery car park, leaving a trail of compost behind us. I always have to over-complicate life. I also found that the effort of bending over, coupled with the overwhelming excitement was starting to bring on a migraine. Flashes of light and tunnel vision: the tell-tale signs. Oh no. I did not want anything to spoil our day. I sat for the rest of the short journey with my hands over my eyes, blocking out the light and willing the monster migraine to disappear. It worked.

By the time, we pulled up outside Jill's beautiful Georgian house it had eased off. We tripped down the front path to the brilliant gleaming red door, We were greeted first by Elsie's booming bark. That's Jill's beautiful, bouncy bearded collie. Following closely behind, our lovely hostess. I thought that perhaps her son, Charlie, might be joining us for lunch, but he lives in Falmouth. It was just the three of us.

Jill made us a delicious salad, which we ate in her tastefully furnished dining room. However, afterwards it was back to the kitchen where we sat chatting comfortably. She is an amazing raconteur, incredibly entertaining and it would be fair to say both Ralph and I were totally bewitched.

Whilst talking, the list of overlapping interests grew longer. We both love writing and drawing, reading, have dyslexic children (who have done very well educationally), demented relatives, and both of us have had breast cancer. We laughed so much with our exchange of dementia tales. She looked after her mum for quite a few years in the annexe in her garden. We are doing a similar thing with Ralph's mum, although not in quite as elegant an annexe as 'The Apple Barn', overlooking her immaculately kept garden. She told us some hilarious stories about her mum's antics. I laughed until I cried.

We didn't leave until 6pm. Considering we'd never actually met before, I felt totally at ease and as though I'd known her all my life. It would seem that the feeling was mutual (or perhaps that's just her gift of putting people at their ease?) Her text to us the day after:

Dear Judith & Ralph

So nice to finally meet you yesterday though I felt as if I'd known you forever. Great to talk about dyslexia & dementia with those who really KNOW. Thanx also for the beautiful tubs of flowers which look perfect on either side of the back door. Hope to see you again soon. Love from Jill xxx

I do hope we get to meet Jill again. I feel as though I have found a replacement for the Gill (my sister and best friend) who I lost to cancer four years ago. Jill definitely has a gift for weaving a spell, not only in her books. Meeting my author heroine has certainly been one of the most memorable and magical days of my life.

In Jill's studio. I didn't get to see her art work but she did show me the proof copy of 'First Prize for the Worst Witch' published in September 2018.

The migraine inducing pots standing guard at Jill's back door, along with the beautiful Elsie.

POSTSCRIPT AUGUST 2021

was very sad to learn from the BBC that the inspirational Jill passed away. She had told ne earlier in the year that cancer had returned and she was 'very scared'. A great loss to ne writing world. **https://en.wikipedia.org/wiki/Jill_Murphy**

THE JOYS OF THE COUNTRYSIDE

A SPRING WALK WITH KEN

Sunday 11 March 2012

Plantlife Walk from Ranscombe Farm

After nearly three years of DIY and very little spare time to enjoy countryside pursuits, it's a real treat to do the simple things in life, like taking a walk in the countryside. My husband and I normally just head off on our own, like we did when it snowed in February. More often than not we find ourselves making for the lovely village of Cobham and the lure of its three, equally lovely, pubs.

We have some spectacular countryside surrounding our own village of Cuxton too. We are lucky to live in an area that has been deemed of 'Special Scientific Interest' due to the rare plants (meadow clary, rough mallow, and fly, lady and man orchids) that grow on the chalk lands. For this reason, Plantlife, manage Ranscombe Farm reserve, in order to safeguard these tiny treasures.

A Plantlife poster outside the butcher's-cum-Post Office advertised a walk around Ranscombe Reserve so I had duly scribbled the details on the calendar. Sunday arrives and drawing back the curtains on a beautiful sunny morning, we would be foolish not to go.

I am glad we did. Ken Laws, who I know from West Kent Downs Countryside Trust was leading the walk. He is extremely knowledgeable about the area, having lived on Dene Court Farm. During my stint on the committee of WKDCT, I remember him telling us that his father was still using traditional farming methods with a horse- drawn plough, right into the 60's.

The small assembled group set off towards Ranscombe Farm. It really is a perfect day for walking. Glancing behind me towards the River Medway, the view is simply breathtaking. Watery sunshine competing with a thin veil of mist creates a truly atmospheric picture – my phone camera 'snap 'doesn't do it justice.

Before we reach the private property of the farm we veer off to the left and follow the track, skirting a field on one side and trees on the other. Ken stops to point out the field where there had been a fictitious airfield during the Second World War and comments:

'Yes, even we had bombs in Cuxton. In August 1944 one doodle bug destroyed part of Ranscombe Farm and the four oast houses. That's why it is a bit of a hotch potch of architectural design. I was only a mere lad then and the other Doodle Bug came down just to the left of Upper Bush. However the impact was still enough to blow the windows out on the primary school in Cuxton. I got the afternoon off school!!'

We emerge onto the slope where Ken points out the evidence of past settlements. A local amateur archaeologist has unearthed thousands of flint heads. Ken shows us a press cutting from the local paper with a photo of a massive flint axe which had been excavated from a garden on the Rochester Road. One of the group exclaims:

'That's the axe which was found in my garden!'

Apparently the professional archaeologist was trying to suggest it was Neanderthal due to its size. Far too big for us mere Homo sapiens but seemingly sparking some controversy in the archaeological world. Whilst we are debating the pedigree of the relics, a buzzard hovers silently overhead. We are obviously too big to be of interest and he glides away in search of smaller prey.

We carry on towards Cobham, puffing our way up the steep slope through the thick woodlands. The birch trees are still bare; only the merest hint of shoots. It's so warm one would think it's the end of spring rather than the beginning. I can really feel those leg muscles pulling, having been very lazy for the last year. Ken is pushing himself up the slope with the aid of a walking stick and complains that he still hasn't got over his knee operation. He points to a pile of blocks to our left, scattered amongst some rather funereal yew trees which look a bit out of place amongst the birch.

'That's the Toe Monument – or what's left of it '

'Oh I've heard of that – so that's where it is' I commented.

Then Ken related the sorry tale:

'Yes, for those of you who don't know the story, this is the Toe Monument erected by Lady Darnley. According to the records, Edward

Bligh, the 5th Earl of Darnley, was walking around his estate in February 1835 with some companions when he saw a woodcutter attacking a tree with his axe. A member of the Earl's staff gave the following account of what the Earl said and did:

' ' Now I'll show you how to cut a root in halves ' and he took the woodcutter's axe, struck hard upon the root when the axe glided off and just caught the little toe of his foot and part of the next thro' his boot. He started and said 'I have just harmed myself, I fear! But it might have been worse and I ought to consider myself fortunate' '

Next day he wrote to a friend saying:

"We are all well here, barring that I almost cut off a little toe with an axe yesterday: providentially it is a matter of no consequence, but might have been a serious accident.' '

Sadly it was a matter of consequence in those days before our modern drugs and tetanus injections. A mere cut could prove fatal. The Earl contracted lockjaw and died three days later.

Although there are only those few stones left of the toe monument (a consequence of mindless vandalism), the rather grander Darnley Mausoleum, has been restored to its former glory. That was our next port of call. The Mausoleum stands proudly on top of the hill overlooking the beautiful lush green woods and fields of the Cobham Estate.

Sadly you can't enter the Mausoleum unless by prior arrangement. A huge perimeter fence surrounds it and then a smaller fence within. The vandals won't wreck it so easily now!

After walking across the hill looking over Cuxton and Upper Bush we are in the woods again and Ken mentions Andre Van Beest, 'the Cuxton hermit' who lived on one of the 'leisure plots' for 16 years. He lived a self-sufficient life, keeping chickens and a goat for milk. According to Ken, he would barter his eggs for other goods in the local shops. Apparently Passmores the local shed company gave him a shed to replace his rather makeshift accommodation and that's when the council started to take an interest in the hermit and evicted him in 1987. Another sad story.

The final 'leg' of our walk takes us to the amazing vista overlooking Brockles Field. Wow! It's another stunning view. An information board (courtesy of Lottery Funding) helpfully indicates the areas of interest. But it's the beautifully carved bench that catches my eye. I wonder who is responsible for this superb handiwork. It's definitely a perfect place to sit and contemplate the view, after admiring (and stroking) the wonderful owl, fox, rabbit, badger and bat carved into the bench.

The group thank Ken enthusiastically, united in their enjoyment of the three hour walk. We promise to go to the beating of the bounds in October; or I hope, before then, to another of the events advertised in the leaflet. They say that some of the best things in life are free and our Plantlife walk is definitely a testament to that.

Green Lanes and Green Men

'Time & Tides' Walk guided

Saturday 11 August 2012

We couldn't have asked for a better weather for the 'Time and Tides' walk around the beautiful green lanes of the Cuxton countryside. I was also rather intrigued - 'Who are the green men?' I asked myself. Did aliens invade us in the distant past?

I was prepared for this walk. Armed with a pad, I was going to scribble down all the Cuxton-related facts. Needless to say, despite my good intentions I was slightly side-tracked gossiping with my friend who had come from Deal to join the walk. I don't seem to be doing too well for the Time & Tides walks as on the 'Curlews, Convicts and Contraband' walk I thought I'd be clever and use the recorder on my phone. Not so clever. I hadn't fully charged my phone before the walk and these blasted Android phones are ravenous beasts and guzzle power. Using the recorder sapped the power in the first fifteen minutes. Even worse, I managed to write down my impressions of the walk once I had returned home and then have closed down my netbook without saving. Not even the hint of a 'recovered document'. The joys of technology! Please transport me back to the days of Dickens and quills!

Fortunately, knowing Carol has paid dividends as she has kindly sent me the notes from her walks, so I am hoping , months later, to be able to do justice to Carol's excellent commentary on that walk. So that's my next writing project.....

For this walk, we set off from the Community Church in Bush Road. I was expecting to see a few familiar faces. The only person I recognized was one German woman who had been on the 'Curlews, Convicts and Contraband' walk. Oh and of course my husband, Ralph, our guide Carol (an acquaintance from the Medway Mermaids writers' group) and my old university friend, Carolyn. Although Carolyn is not local (lives in Little Mongeham, Deal) she loves walking and has only had one walk in Cuxton, to admire the restored Darnley Mausoleum.

After the short introduction, Carol led us up the steep pathway through the woods to St Michael's Church. The series of steps are killers and most of us were puffing by the time we reached the graveyard. Oh well if any of us keel over with a fatal heart attack, we're in the right place! After a chance to catch our breath Carol explained the origins of the name Cuxton:

'The name dates back to Anglo Saxon times when the settlement was known as Cucola's Stone or Cuclestane. Cucola was probably a local chieftain and the stone was the boundary marker of his territories. The stone may well have been here in the churchyard, as this has been a place of worship for thousands of years. Beneath the church there are even the remains of a Roman villa and it is likely that it was a place of Pagan worship prior to the Romans and Christianity. Early churches were often built at locations where people already met for worship and the presence of an earlier building may explain the strange alignment of the church on south-east orientation, an ancient rhyme records this 'If you would see a church misspent then you must go to Cuxton in Kent'.'

Carol paused, shepherding us into the church. I hesitated on the threshold, as there was another member of our party that I didn't mention - Suki, our fluffy white Bichon Frisse companion. However, one of our group urged me inside:

'Oh bring the dog in I'm sure ***He*** *won't mind'*

Once inside the small Norman church, our eyes adjusted to the gloom. The beautiful stained glass windows glittered and dazzled; the intense beams of sunlight illuminating the images with a religious reverence. The Victorians stamped their mark on the church with these multi-coloured biblical depictions, although personally I like the simplicity of the original understated Norman windows.

Carol continued her narrative, pointing to one of the windows on the left hand side of the church. Finally the Green Man explained

'Can you see engraved in the stone, there's a face?'

We all strained our eyes to see it.

'That's the Green Man, who was a Pagan fertility symbol. A lot of the old Pagan deities were incorporated into the Christian settings to make the new religion more acceptable.'

Well that's the mystery of the Green Man solved. However, she continued with an even more bizarre tale:

'There's a story about a glass coffin in the church. Allegedly, in 1783 a glass coffin was the last resting place of Margaret Cousins. The coffin was on display in the church. Apparently, Margaret feared being buried alive. She consequently left explicit instructions that on her death she must be buried in a glass coffin that had a key left inside. Although after about almost 100 years it was apparent that she was well and truly dead and was transferred to the graveyard in 1868. I did have a look the other day to see if I could find a gravestone for her but couldn't see one. Does anyone know if there is a gravestone?'

She scanned the group for an affirmative but everyone looked blank. Perhaps the glass coffin story is just one of those local myths?

We left the gloom of the church and emerged into the brilliant sunshine. Without doubt, it is one of the best days of this otherwise disappointing summer.

We followed Carol along another shady, inclining pathway leading out onto a large field, overlooking the River Medway. You could see the unrelenting A2 traffic snaked and glimmered, slithering its way through the green and yellow patchwork over the majestic road bridge and on towards the coast. A herd of bullocks chewed the cud just casting us a brief glance, although Carol did warn us they could be a bit frisky and inquisitive, so to be on our guard.

Carol guided us through the woods, pointing out interesting flora and fauna. We also have some rare orchids that only grow on chalk lands, which we have in abundance in Medway but sadly, we didn't see any orchids. However, it's amazing the diversity of the wild flowers and their medicinal properties.

'Look at that' she said pointing to a small plant growing under the

hedgerow 'That's wild marjoram. Our ancestors used to take it to prevent deafness. Over there is St John's Wort – a cure for depression, melancholy and madness'

Perhaps she could have recommended something for near choking incidents. Carolyn was so busy telling us about her recent Club Med holiday that a short-sighted fly invaded her mouth. Much coughing and spluttering ensued. Or perhaps Carolyn could have eaten some St John's Wort. She was pretty mad with that fly and I don't suppose the fly was too happy either.

Finally, we came out of the woods and I recognized where we were. One of my favourite local haunts – Upper Bush. Two or three years back it was my regular running destination, before my knees started to creak. I've often fancied living in a hamlet – the ultimate rural retreat. It was a bigger community originally but over time dwindled to five cottages when Cuxton became the local hub of activity. If I won the lottery I would love to live in the chocolate-box Tudor-built 'High Birch Cottage', with its traditional English garden at the front and sweeping expanse of immaculate lawn at the back. I mistakenly thought it was the oldest of the cottages. In fact, I was surprised to learn that the original part of the extended 'Barrow Hill Cottage' is older and goes back to 1390. There might be an ancient burial site nearby as barrow is the ancient name for a funeral mound. We also learnt that Upper Bush was originally called Birch – hence the name Birch Cottage.

Then back along the path that brought us to Upper Bush, taking a right down the valley. We stopped at another scenic view overlooking the Dene valley. The Acheulian people are believed to be the original inhabitants. They used flint in a sophisticated way. Carol handed us a flint to examine. The edges are still as sharp as they were when the Acheulians used them over 200,000 years ago! We continued through the middle of a field, brushing against the tall ripening ears of wheat. Suki was clearly not happy. It must have appeared to her to be an endless tunnel. Not to mention the noisy rumble of the combine harvester in the distance. She was also irritated by the wheat stalks. They attached themselves like Velcro to her thick fur. We tried to hurry her along and offer her some soothing words of reassurance. We could see clouds of dust billowing over the golden stubble of the harvester's handiwork. Definitely a rural idyll - or at least I thought so until the combine harvester finally came into view – it was a monster. The huge rotating red blades glinted menacingly in the sunshine. The ferocious machine would rip anything in its pathway to shreds. Our fluffy friend was right to be alarmed!

We stopped for breath at the end of the field. Carol talked about the harvesting traditions and how the Corn Dolly was a sign of fertility and generally fed the horse in the days of the horse drawn plough.

We weaved back in a circular route along the upper path of the woods. It was eerily quiet with just the gentle hum of the M2 traffic in the distance. The canopy of oak, beech, and hornbeam stretched their branches towards the life-giving sun.

Carol stopped to point out some of the wild plants and related more interesting snippets:

'Here we have the royals of the forest. 'She pointed out two different trees:

'For the druids Queen Beech was the Consort to King Oak. Beech leaves also have medicinal properties – they made poultices for swellings and from the bark made tar to help alleviate bronchitis. Oak trees were considered sacred, as the druids believed a druid spirit lived within. It was therefore considered unlucky to cut an oak down'

Obviously not the case now – where we would be without our fashionable oak furniture? Not to mention the fleets of oak ships, in previous centuries.

'Oak is also host to mistletoe, which was considered to have magical properties, no doubt giving rise to kissing under the mistletoe at Christmas. Druids considered Yews as sacred. They have long been associated with religion. Probably because fallen branches easily root and regrow, becoming a symbol of rebirth. Those small plants over there are wood avens. They're a sign of ancient woodland. They were commonly used for stomach ailments such as colic. They were also used as a spring tonic and boiled in wine to help a cold brain!'

Now that's what I call a good excuse for a glass of wine.....a chilly brain!

'Acorns were believed to protect you from lightening! That's why you see acorns carved in woodwork and newel posts. Also, if you keep an acorn in your purse it will keep you young. '

Scrap the botox - let's just fill up our purses with acorns instead!

'Hornbeam is a native tree– it's a very strong wood which was used by the Romans for their chariot wheels. Hornbeam has also been used originally for cogs and also the hammers in pianos The leaves in past times were used for their medicinal qualities – useful for helping to get rid of blisters and also brewed to make a spring tonic.'

All too soon we were back at St Michael's Church. Now it was downhill all the way. Thank goodness those steep steps into Wood Street aren't so bad on the way down. We said our goodbyes at the Community Church and headed off home for our barbecue lunch. There's nothing like a two and a half hour walk to build up an appetite for burgers.

I'm really sorry the Time & Tides Project is coming to an end as I would have liked to have been more involved. Thanks must go to the Icon Theatre and Nicola Waddington for organizing this thoroughly interesting project and of course to Carol for making the walk so enjoyable.

Watercolour inspired by one of our many trips to Howletts Zoo

THE JOYS OF WILDLIFE

THE JOY OF ZOOS

I have been wondering if there is a possibility of doing a TV programme called 'The Zoo Inspector'. I rather fancy being the Alex Polizzi of the zoo world. I am sure there are people that vet zoos (pardon the pun) but I think there is a role for a "mystery visitor" who gives the zoos a rating from the visitor perspective.

I have actually built up quite a portfolio of visits to zoos, wildlife parks, nature reserves and sanctuaries over the years. I have a particular soft spot for Howletts. I have visited this zoo more than 20 times, over the years. I even had a passport a couple of years ago.

I have put them in order of my absolute favourites:
Sepilok (Borneo Malaysia), Tanjung Putting National Park (East Kalimantan, Indonesia), Kruger National Park (South Africa), Elephant Place (Port Elizabeth, South Africa), Singapore Zoo (both night & day Zoo), Howlett's (near Canterbury, Kent), Woburn (Bedfordshire) Colchester (Essex), Port Lympne (near Hythe, Kent), Woburn, Dublin, Whipsnade, Longleat, East Midlands, Wingham Wildlife Park (Kent), London Zoo, Monkey World (Dorset), Paignton, Chiang Mai, Bangkok, Kuala Lumpur, Tenerife's Monkey World, Paris and Helsinki.

I am hoping Helsinki's improved since the time we visited in 2001. It was an awful zoo. It reminded me of London Zoo when I visited it in the 60's. It was literally a grey concrete jungle. Having been to London Zoo in the past few years, it is much improved. Far more green and leafy these days!

There are still a couple of zoos on my "to see" list. The Durrell Zoo in Jersey and The Big Cat Sanctuary in Kent.

Of course I must also mention my favourite local zoo of the moment- The Fenn Bell Inn Conservation Project (or as I call it – 'The Zoo at Hoo'). It's only 15 minutes from our house at St Mary Hoo. It's a total delight and the best thing of all – it's attached to a pub, where we have had a few decent lunches. We particularly like their lemurs.

Check it out. The entrance fee is very low.

www.fennbellinn.co.uk

or its Facebook page seems to be kept more up to date than the website. You'll find it under 'The Fenn Bell Conservation project'

CLOSE ENCOUNTERS OF THE MONKEY KIND

I've always been a bit of an ape fancier ever since my teenage visits to Howlett's Zoo in Kent. The gorillas were totally enthralling and occasionally John Aspinall, Howlett's owner, would interact with his extended family on their home turf. Their cage.

One such encounter ended with John flat on his back after a game of 'swinging the tyre' catapulted him off his feet. A moment's inattention meant one mischievous silver back had the last laugh and at the same time asserted his authority as the alpha male. Despite the obvious dangers of playing with such powerful relatives, I was so envious of those close encounters. Consequently, those regular trips got me hooked.

Therefore, for the amateur ape fancier a trip to Sepilok, Borneo was definitely high up on the top 10 monkey chart. The largest orangutan sanctuary in the world is a lush tropical forest reserve. Orphaned orangutans undergo rehabilitation there. They are also protected from their biggest predator on earth. Us. Too much of the orangutan's domain has been decimated by our need for oil. In this case, palm oil. Vast swathes of palm oil plantations now replace the orangutans old stomping ground.

Making our way along the wooden creaky walkway, above the dense vegetation we can only imagine the multitude of life scurrying amongst the undergrowth: millipedes, scorpions, beetles, ants, frogs and lizards all busy and unseen on the forest floor. Heady warm scents assault our noses: damp leaves, moist wood and that delicious fungal overtone.

High up in the leafy canopy we glimpse a trace of ruddy-brown glistening in the sun's early rays. The wild old men were comfortable in their lofty domain, lounging on branches as if they were hammocks.

However, from their vantage point, as soon as they spied the two rangers with their bulging carrier bags, full of delicious tropical fruit, they were on the move. It's an amazing spectacle. Our nearest (and probably hairiest) relative swings so effortlessly through the trees. Within minutes, they were dropping onto the feeding platform, like seasoned paratroopers. A mature orangutan slapped one of the rangers on the back, perhaps in greeting or maybe as a rebuke for a slow breakfast delivery.

From the viewing platform, we watched the busy mouths quickly demolishing the lychees, rambutans and bananas. The younger cheekier ones soon get bored with the eating rituals and either poked and prodded at their peers, instigating a game of tag or irritating the adults who give them a swift cuff around the ear. Unexpectedly a large orangutan caused excitement by joining us on the viewing platform. The noisy thud of his leap from the trees took everyone by surprise. He obviously wanted to get up close and personal with us too. He was close enough to touch. He didn't stay long enough for a cuddle and was off swinging back through the trees, full stomach bulging. An aerial performer, par excellence.

Even more fascinating was watching the pecking order at work. The elders claiming their fill first, followed by the youngsters and then at the lower end of the spectrum, the much smaller macaque monkeys tentatively creeping up from underneath the platform and trying to craftily swipe the odd banana or lychee. One was even trying to pull a banana through a slat in the platform. Once the orangutans ate their fill they dispersed as quickly as they arrived, leaving the macaques to clean up. The last remnants of fruit gone, the macaques turned their sights to us human stragglers still on the viewing platform. One Dutch woman sat next to the wooden railing where several macaque mothers with their tiny babies seemed quite happy to pose for the cameras. She didn't quite expect such close attention from one of the juvenile macaques. It jumped on her shoulder whipping off her hair band and with its long delicate fingers rifled through her tresses looking for nits. She was starting to look decidedly uncomfortable with the whole process, as she didn't want to provoke a bite from those vicious looking teeth. The 'audience' however found it all highly amusing and were so engrossed that no one noticed a rather bold macaque edging up to the woman's rucksack lying on the decking. Luckily, my husband clocked the attempted mugging out of the corner of his eye.

'Oi' he shouted. Despite the bag's overwhelming size, the cheeky macaque had no intention of abandoning his booty. My husband grabbed at the bag and a tug of war ensued. The perpetrator chattered aggressively, baring his teeth menacingly but eventually gave in to the hero of the hour, my alpha male.

A macaque investigating a plastic bag. Sadly too much human debris carelessly discarded.

My monkey friends in Krabi, Thailand

For a different monkey experience, I highly recommend the 'Adventure of a Lifetime' video on Youtube:

https://www.youtube.com/watch?v=QtXby3twMmI

PYGMY !

Two eyes are blazing fury. Ears flap in warning; the grey bulk charges from the dense undergrowth bordering the Kinabatangan River in Borneo. Supposedly a pygmy, at eight feet tall, it towers over our boat. There's a serious possibility that it might become the ninth uninvited passenger in our small launch.

We certainly hadn't been expecting such an encounter when we met the rest of our group that morning. Bleary-eyed and rubbing sleep from our eyes, we boarded our eight-seater vessel for our first dawn trip. 06.00 and it is dark and chilly. The river is swathed eerily in mist. It's reminiscent of a scene from the film, 'Apocalypse Now'. Snatches of, 'Flight of the Valkyries' infiltrate my brain ominously. No helicopters though.... just the cacophony of night-time jungle sounds. Hoots, screeches and whoops reverberate through the cool muggy air.

Our boat putters along the dark river, Leo our guide, flashing his powerful torch. He catches the reflection of a set of eyes...the elusive leopard cat. Then the torch beam locks onto two proboscis monkeys, cuddled up on an overhanging branch. They slumber on, blissfully unaware. The boat's spotlight catches slim silhouettes in the river. A family of otters glide gracefully through the murky waters of the Mananggul River, a tributary of the Kinabatangan. Our boat tries to keep up with these master swimmers but they evade us, leaping onto the bank and scampering off into the undergrowth.

Light seeps into the darkness; the mist evaporates. Leo points to other wildlife, starting to stir in the warm glow of dawn.

'Look over there!' He points to two stork-billed kingfishers on the same tree. Malaysia, and its Island territory of Borneo, has a huge array of wildlife; so many types of kingfisher: common, collared, blue collared, blue eared, chestnut collared, oriental dwarf, ruddy, sacred and white throated. Borneo seems to have more than its fair share.

This stork-billed kingfisher is the largest though and stretches out on its tropical perch, positively proud of its status. Various other bird life swoop into our field of vision; we are treated to egrets, buffy fish owls and hawks.

A wild boar snuffles around for tasty treats on the edges of the muddy banks. It's keeping its distance from the glassy-eyed crocodile, wallowing just below the water's surface. The croc is eyeing up the boar as his potential breakfast treat. Bacon, lovely! I'm sure I saw him licking his lips in anticipation. We move on before any 'boaring' drama unfolds.

Silver-coated monkeys, chattering noisily overhead, catch our attention. They perform their daily aerial aerobics with ease. Wan, our driver stops the boat; captivated, we watch with rapt attention. A make-shift picnic breakfast is distributed by Leo: tea, coffee, biscuits, bread, butter and jam. The Anchor butter seems a bit incongruous in this setting; we are 100 kms from real civilisation.

Continuing along the river, we scan the leafy canopy. We hold our breath....could that be....yes it is. There in the distance is a glimpse of glistening amber, the jewel in Borneo's crown: the orang-utan. Excitement ripples through the boat as we reach for cameras, or in our case...don't. Our camera has run out of power. Both Sean and Caroline have heavy-duty cameras with telephoto lenses. Hopefully they'll get some good shots, even though the orang-utan is about 200 yards away. They have promised to share their photographic booty with us by e-mail.

The distant, though brief, glimpse is special, even though we had a much closer encounter at Sepilok, the orang-utan reserve. One shaggy adult had ambled across the viewing platform, totally at ease with his human counterparts. Too trusting. We, his descendants, have ripped down much of his forest territory; replaced it with vast tracts of palm oil plantations for our benefit. Somehow that doesn't sit comfortably with me. Awe and guilt are in equal measure. I eat Olivio, and no doubt hundreds of other products, containing palm oil. If I and my fellow humans don't change our ways, all this wonderful forest will be gone.

Now our attention is distracted by sounds from the bank, noisy cracking and snapping, large feet trampling reeds and bushes. We catch a glimpse of grey. Leo, in his wisdom, whispers:

'There they are...the pygmies. We might be able to get a closer look.'

The pygmies he's referring to are the local breed of elephants. He ties the boat to a tree. Climbing out, followed closely by Shaun and Emma, they are half way up the bank when one of the elephants charges from the bushes. He's not my idea of a pygmy. My heart misses a beat as Leo, Shaun and Emma slip down the bank into the mud, then clamber, panic-stricken, onto the boat.

The "pygmy" looks none too pleased. His blazing eyes convey the message. We are on his territory and need to respect that fact. We humans don't always heed the warnings.

This might be our wake up call.

Coombe Hayes Barn – Uplyme – Dorset
Spring 2011

After the success of our first HOGS (Honor Oak Girls Grammar School) weekend away last March to the Cotswold's, it seemed like a good idea to make it an annual event. Last year it was the hard core Kent contingent – Penny, Sandra, Anne. Claire and yours truly. We had such fun, laughing hysterically and releasing copious amounts of endorphins. It was a spa for the soul and better than any therapy or counselling session. Probably a lot cheaper too!

I was very keen for another trip. It was like the school journey that I never had. There were trips away but rather exotic choices – I remember the more wealthy pupils swanning off for skiing in Switzerland or on a Cruise to the Netherlands. Anyone would have thought we went to an exclusive girl's private school rather than a Grammar School in Peckham! I would have been happy with a trip to the Isle of Wight, which I considered to be very exotic when I was a youngster.

Last year had been difficult after the Cotswold's weekend. A couple of weeks prior my mum had been admitted to hospital. Two weeks after the Cotswold trip my mum died. This came as a huge shock. Although she was very frail, we expected the hospital to fix her up and send her home. The rest of the year was spent sorting out her affairs and crying a lot. I was experiencing a deep seated numbness despite my cheery exterior. I felt like a 50-something orphan.

Christmas was particularly difficult and I had to make a real effort to do all the normal Christmassy things. I couldn't really pay much attention to the possible HOGS trip away, so was very grateful when Penny took the initiative to research a suitable venue. She gave three options but as no one could make a decision. Penny made it for us and booked a superb (if somewhat expensive) cottage in Uplyme, outside Lyme Regis, Dorset. We optimistically believed we might have 8 of us this time, so the cottage she chose would sleep 8 comfortably but up to 12. However, we were 5 again but instead of Claire, another friend, Jackie, joined us. Jackie had left our school in the 3rd year when her parents had to move to Eastbourne. Only Penny had seen Jackie since she had left school and that was only in the last year. The rest of the group hadn't seen her for 40 years. I remember her as a pretty, petite, dark-haired, shy and nervous girl. It would be interesting to meet the grown up Jackie. She lives in West Sussex but commutes 3 days a week to work in Bristol. So she agreed she would make her own way to Uplyme from Bristol.

Anne, Penny, Sandra and I agreed to travel in one car. With the ridiculous price of petrol at £1.39 a litre (or more), you need to have a full car these days! I had agreed to drive.

Just 30 minutes before we were due to leave a panic call from Sandra:

'Judith, I'm really sorry but I've just spoken to my mum and my dad is having difficulty breathing so she's rung for an ambulance. I really need to go and support them so I will not be travelling with you. I'm hoping to join you later once I've satisfied myself that he's OK as this has happened before.'

'Are you absolutely sure, Sandra? We could delay our departure to wait for you? Particularly as you had a long journey to Eastbourne yesterday.' Sandra had been to Sue Wood's mum's funeral just the day before. Sue had originally intended to come away with us.

I was disappointed that Sandra wouldn't be travelling with us and didn't like to think of her undertaking the 3 ½ hour journey alone. But she is both a very conscientious and determined woman, so there was no way I was going to dissuade her.

Penny arrived on time. I was packed and ready to go despite my almost OCD need to clean the house from top to bottom before I go away on trips lasting more than 12 hours! It drives my husband nuts.

She parked her Mercedes sports car on our cramped driveway.

'Sorry about the state of the car' she apologized 'my car is filthy within minutes down our country road. Perhaps Ralph will clean it for me?' Fat chance. He hasn't cleaned our cars for at least two years but then complains when I take them to the Cuxton Car Wash! We bundled Penny's bags into the back of my ample boot. I have come to the conclusion that at this stage of my life everything has to be ample.

Next port of call was Anne's house in Chalk. As Anne teaches, she was officially meant to be in school until 3pm but managed to slide off at 1.30pm not having lessons in the afternoon.

She was hopping up and down on her front step with bags piled up ready for the off.

'How long are we going away, Anne?' I asked. We had enough food for a week. Anne is definitely a feeder.

I had foolishly offered to drive. Last year I was the nominated navigator. With Anne driving. Several times in that role I was reminded that I should be looking at the map and not distracted by the giggling "girls" in the back seat. All rather reminiscent of school but Anne now instead of the serious schoolgirl has transformed into seriously bossy school mistress. I will no doubt revert to being recalcitrant pupil and class clown. To be honest, I would have been happier to be a passenger in the back gossiping. I am, in my book, a perfect passenger. I always have complete confidence in the person driving or where there are any confidence issues just close my eyes and go to sleep! However, I thought it might be easier to be driver than navigator.

Wrong!

Major faux pas. Or perhaps I should say "poofwaah". That's my husband's very own malapropism for any mishap. Although I travel along the A2 at least 3 times a week, I rarely join the M25 at the Dartford Junction. A moment's distraction (too much chit chat) and I found my car merrily driving itself over the bridge towards the Dartford Tunnel.

'Oh effing hell' I exclaimed (quite politely I thought) when I realised I was committed. Where was my trusty navigator? Too busy chatting with Penny. Perhaps the Sat Nav might have been more reliable after all? I was so annoyed with myself and even more irritated by the long snaking queue which we were forced to join.

'Oh well' Anne said, breezily 'we can get off at the next junction, can't we?' After ten minutes or so we managed to get off the approach road. We crossed the bridge in order to join the M25 going southbound. Not sure how I managed it (again where was my navigator?) but we ended back on the M25 northbound and this time there was no escaping the gaping jaw of the tunnel. There was a cry of disbelief from Penny in the back seat.

'On no! We're going to be really late now. Poor Jackie will get there before us and I was hoping we would be there first.'

I just laughed, feeling more than a tad sheepish. It took us about 20 minutes and £3.00 of needless toll fees to go through the tunnel and back again into yet another queue of traffic over the QE2 Bridge. I tried to put a positive slant on the unfortunate escapade by saying:

'Oh never mind. It's not the end of the world. Jackie's a big girl and she won't be standing on the doorstep waiting for us, will she? This will no doubt become one of those anecdotal moments...and I am sure it was meant to be.'

Luckily we had no other major diversions or hold ups for most of the journey, just a very short wee stop at Fleet Services. There was however a very nasty accident which had closed part of the opposite side of the A35. I steadfastly hold onto the tenet that 'everything is for a reason' very much in the same naïve way that Voltaire's Candide believes that 'all is for the best in the best of all possible worlds'. I can only assume that we missed death or mutilation by our Dartford Tunnel detour.

We knew we would arrive at Lyme Regis in the dark but we weren't reckoning on any additional difficulties in finding our cottage. So the fog was less than welcome. It started to get misty when we were about 45 minutes away from our destination. It was worse in certain spots, slowing us down to a crawl. We arrived later than expected in Lyme Regis and finding the cottage in Uplyme was not an easy proposition. We had to stop at a cottage to ask directions. It was a VERY narrow winding lane, so we kept our fingers crossed that we met no oncoming traffic. They wouldn't see us very easily in the fog and my husband would not be best pleased if I returned with a damaged car.

Finally we found the well disguised lane, which would have been difficult to find even without the fog. We clunked our way over the cattle grid described in the directions and along a pot holed rough track. It was worth the search. Even in the foggy darkness the place looked beautiful from the outside. Jackie was already there and finally we met after 40 years.

The years rolled back in an instant. There we were, full of excitement, five gaggling thirteen year olds again.

'Jackie...oh my god you've hardly changed at all' we said in unison. She was still as petite as ever, wrinkle-free and not a grey hair in sight. I felt positively like the incredible hulk towering over her. Poor Jackie ...she'd been waiting hours. Luckily she isn't that fussed about food (unless chocolate is the major constituent) whereas we were all starving and had roles been reversed we would have been gnawing at the kitchen table!

Before unpacking and starting dinner, we explored the cottage. Three bedrooms upstairs – two twins and one with a superb four poster (and cot – as if we needed that!). Also a very spacious bathroom complete with double sink.

Downstairs was a very beautifully appointed kitchen with a huge expensive range and a table seating twelve with no problem. Shame there are only the five of us, as this is the ultimate party cottage. The lounge is vast with big comfy leather sofas, a couple of other easy chairs and a rather ancient wood burner. Everything is very tastefully furnished with an eclectic mix of old and contemporary furniture. It really is home from home...or at least (for some of us) that aspirational home we'd love to live in. I'd move in tomorrow if the owners didn't object.

From the lounge, a corridor lined with opening glass doors on one side that led into the heated swimming pool. The corridor also acted as a kind of games rooms with a table football and a lovely old cabinet housing PC and Playstation. Definitely a house the kids would love.

Peering through the windows to the pool, we could see it was situated in what would have originally been the courtyard. It had a conservatory type structure built over it which connected the cottage to what had once been the stable block. Now the horses' home had been tastefully transformed into two gorgeous bedrooms. Both had lovely features - one having a gallery/loft housing two more single beds. A great family room. The other room had sky lights, an upper door to the hay loft and a window overlooking the corridor, pool and a small indoor flower bed. Such lovely touches. Both rooms had immaculate, contemporary ensuite toilet and shower rooms. I think I can say we were more than impressed.....

The next important item on the agenda was a much needed cup of tea and a catch up with Jackie to find out what she had been doing in the intervening forty years. We could have ended up with no dinner, distracted by the conversation. Luckily, our very own Mary Poppins, Penny, had brought the precooked ingredients for a lasagne. I brought the salad....and numerous bottles of wine. I get my priorities right. Jackie had brought her own food as she has a very specific diet that includes a lot of chocolate products. I must say I must try the Jackie diet. She looks exceptionally good on it.

The four of us sat at the huge table and ate our delicious dinner, exchanging stories. Anne, Penny and I have the advantage, having caught up on each other's lives over the last 8 years or so. Caroline, the ghost at the table, had reunited about three quarters of our class through her meticulous detective work with the help of Friends Reunited and the web. There was a lot of discussion about Caroline, our missing friend, who sadly died almost two years ago after a long battle with cancer. She was a remarkable person, with a mischievous, intellectual wit who we felt had never really fulfilled her true potential. She had married early, had six children and been trapped in an abusive relationship. The internet had been her escape and right up until the last few weeks of her life, we all received almost daily e-mails from Caroline. Often random links to an article she had read online, or a poem or one of her observations. She enriched everyone's lives and was generous despite having little material wealth. I think we have all kept her e-mails in special folder marked "Caroline" and someone will at some point write her story. Anne was Caroline's closest friend. More like the sister Caroline never had. However, I think she will find it too painful to recount. I guess it will probably be me.

We finally adjourned to the lounge, settling in the squashy sofas. Penny had got the wood burner going, giving the room a warm cosy glow. Sandra had sent a text to Penny an hour or so earlier and we thought her ETA may be about 1.30 am. She had told us not to wait up but we had visions of her losing her way in the foggy, dark Dorset countryside. We couldn't allow that. In any case we were too engrossed in hearing Jackie's story:

'When I left Honor Oak to go to Eastbourne, I was distraught. I think I must have cried for two years. I did settle in eventually but was never really comfortable. Although I stayed on for A-levels I didn't enjoy it at all and left after the first term. I didn't really know what I wanted to do but as I was quite good at maths and my dad was a Bank Manager it made sense to follow him into the banking world. I certainly enjoyed it and was there for 22 years. I hadn't met anyone who I really had a lasting relationship with and I was quite happy on my own with my own house. However, I went away on holiday when I was 34 and met "the man". I knew he was the one and warned my parents that there might be a wedding in the offing. He proposed three days after we came back. We married within 3 months."

'Ahhh how romantic' we chorused. However, the full story was cut short when Penny's mobile rang.

'Where are you Sandra? You think you're quite close but not sure where the lane is? OK we'll come and find you'. Without a moment's hesitation, Anne and I grabbed our coats and shoes, disappearing into the cold dark night in search of our friend. It was a scene reminiscent of the "X files", pitch black and swirling mist. Anne raced off, whilst I was getting the torch from the car's glove box.

'Where are you Anne?'

The torch was worse than useless in the mist. It was all very spooky with a hint of the X-files about it. I really think this could be a setting for a very chilling psychological thriller. I made mental notes that I must use this situation for my next short story.

I eventually found Anne waiting at the end of the track, feeling her way by scuffing her feet on the tarmac. We managed to navigate our way; negotiating the cattle grid in the dark was interesting. Once on the twisting lane we could see the beams from Sandra's headlights further up the hill.

Her car eventually came to a halt at the lane once she saw our shadowy figures. It seems she had already had a bit of a scare by three deer leaping into the road and now two dears with torch! She agreed she would have not found the cottage without our help.

We finally went to bed at 03.30, after showing Sandra the cottage and deciding where we were sleeping. I was in one of the twin beds upstairs but despite a very long day couldn't sleep. My brain was racing and then cramp in my feet made me shoot out of bed and hop around the room. By 5am exhaustion set in and I finally fell asleep.

Not for long though. By 07.00 I was awake. Drawing open the curtains, the watery spring sunshine flooded the room. The view was breath-taking; beautiful green rolling hills scattered with the occasional house or farm.

One by one the tired HOGS girls crept into the kitchen for their reviving early morning drinks. Needless to say breakfast was a leisurely affair, followed by a swim in the pool. It's amazing how ladies can swim and chat at the same time! We had to stagger the showering, so I lingered in the pool a bit longer. At least I could have a good old splash about on my own without being told off. My orca the whale impressions don't go down so well in a small pool.

Finally showered, dressed and hair straightened, we all climbed into the Zafira to explore the delights of Lyme Regis. My husband was quite convinced I must have been there before but as I drove down the hill into the town I knew this was new territory.

We managed to find a place in the busy car park on the front then meandered on foot along the High Street, diving into the interesting shops along the way. The one full of fossils and crystals was not to be missed. The charity shops were a must too and both Anne and I made the obligatory purchases. A shop displaying original pictures in the window also caught our eye. Particularly in my case as the glass artworks were made by a Melanie Boorman. I bought some beautiful glass coasters thinking they may have been made by her too but I suspect they were probably "Made in China".

All the window shopping and walking along the front is very thirst inducing. We soon had to stop for refreshments. The drinks stop then stretched into a lunch stop. It was far too pleasant to move. Here we were sitting outside in the sunshine under a SUN umbrella, overlooking the beautiful British Riviera. In March. Who would have thought it? We were of course wearing our coats and not sporting bikinis.

We wandered leisurely back to the car. By this time it was after 4pm and we were starting to feel chilled as the sun had disappeared. We found our way back to the cottage without too much difficulty in the light, parking in the open garage next to the cottage. We had a couple of hours before going out.

It was Penny's idea to book The Canteen at River Cottage in Axminster for dinner as she had been there before. As I was obviously looking a bit jaded, she suggested we book a taxi so that no one had to drive. The taxi driver drove like a demon though and poor Jackie was flinching all the way. She only flinched a few times when I drove!

It was only once we were at the River Cottage (owned by Hugh Fearnley-Whittingstall or I prefer his nickname – Hugh Fearlessly-Eatsitall) that we realized the food on offer might not suit Jackie as it was all a bit exotic. I had razor clams, chorizo in red wine sauce and fish for main course. Jackie skipped the entrée and dinner; no messing – she went straight for the chocolate pudding. The waiter found that amusing. No doubt Jackie's rejection of the carefully crafted menu will filter through to the great celebrity chef.

We got back to the cottage before 11pm. After a bit of chit chat, we embarked on a game of Logos, which Penny had brought with her. It's a sort of Trivial Pursuit of the marketing world. Great fun and we certainly laughed a lot and learnt a few interesting facts. In all my years in the travel business I never knew Fray Bentos was an actual place. It's in Uruguay!

Tiredness eventually caught up with us all. Anne was the first to flake out on the sofa. We were all glad to get to our beds by one am.

Just as I was drifting off to sleep, there was a torrential deluge of rain making the panes rattle in their frames. We knew that the good weather was not likely to last and the forecast for Sunday was not promising, but perhaps the rain would be during the night and we would wake to another glorious day.

After a really good night's sleep, I was the first one up again. I drew back the curtains and was greeted by……rain. Shame!

We didn't rush over breakfast. We exchanged some of the trials and tribulations in our lives. I shared my frustrations of being only a part-time mum, particularly when my husband and I separated. Some of our skeletons were not for public airing, so they remain confidential to us 'HOGS on tour.'

It would have been tempting to stay at the breakfast table until we left for home. Yet why come all this way and not see the sights? The rain had stopped too, so after the obligatory swim and scramble for the showers, we headed off to Charmouth. The "Gateway to the Jurassic Coast" is only a couple of miles away from the cottage. The sun had emerged from its cloudy blanket and with it the fossil hunters who were busily rooting about in the pebbles looking for prized ancient treasures. It didn't seem the right conditions – we found nothing. We checked with the "professionals". They hadn't found any either. We retreated to the shop; no lack of fossils in there! Ammonites, belemnites, preserved plesiosaurs and tiny insects encased in their tombs of amber. A cornucopia of everything prehistoric. We admired some of the amazing finds ("for display purposes only"), examined the wares on offer – coasters made from polished cross sections of rock, fridge magnets and jewellery. Some purchases were made.....or not, as in Anne's case. We were halfway across the car park when we heard:

'Oi stop thief!' We looked round, the shopkeeper running towards us, waving his arms and looking most indignant. Surely not us? He pointed at Anne, stating:

'I think you've got something you haven't paid for.' Anne looked bemused then flustered when he pointed at her wrist. She had a necklace draped over it.

'Oh no, I'm really sorry. I forgot to pay for the necklace I was going to buy for Jo.' He frog marched her back to the shop, trying to suppress his own mirth, whilst we were hooting with laughter. When she returned to the car, rather sheepishly, we debated whether we would allow a criminal into the car.

We had been debating whether to get a cup of tea in Charmouth but after that embarrassing moment we left rapidly heading for Bridport instead. It was a bit disappointing as most of the town closes on Sunday. Even the café was closing, so we headed to a gastro-style pub instead on the main street and had a well-deserved cup of tea. Bridport is in my consciousness as I thought they held a literary festival each year. However, on reflection it's the prestigious Bridport Prize I'm thinking of. The competition closing date is 31 May, so plenty of time to think about a possible entry!

Reluctantly we wend our way back to the cottage (a bit of a back track in my opinion), pack our bags into our respective cars and say our farewells. I finally met the owners of this rather spectacular cottage when I hand back the key. They were a very friendly couple in their early forties, who have been lucky enough to own the property for 10 years.

We set off for home in the fading light and had an uneventful journey back. I was quite tempted to make a detour to the Dartford Tunnel, just for comic effect. I thought better of it though. I don't think the joke would have been appreciated at ten o'clock at night when we were desperate to get home to our families/husbands/lovers and catch up on our sleep....or not as the case might be!

AS I CANNOT FIND ANY PHOTOS FROM THIS TRIP, IF YOU WANT TO LOOK AT THIS FABULOUS PROPERTY, THE LINK IS:

https://www.cottages.com/cottages/coombehayes-barn-dqs

INTRODUCING A FRIEND ALONG THE ROAD AT RANSCOMBE FARM RESERVE

RANDOM

JOYS

THE JOY OF DYSLEXIA

Written December 2017

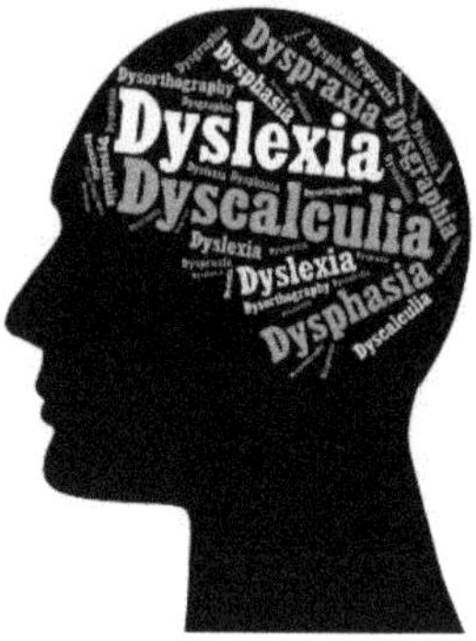

I'm sure many people (particularly dyslexics) will be puzzled by the title of this piece.

What joy is there in dyslexia?

Well, in truth, probably not too much joy at all for those who struggle with both reading and writing.

My connection with the dyslexia world has come about mainly through Amelia, my dyslexic daughter. Despite the struggles I witnessed when she was a youngster, she has overcome many of her dyslexic difficulties by sheer hard work, determination and the help of some great teachers.

I recognised she had problems quite early on. It was probably as young as three or four. She couldn't repeat rhymes and would get her words muddled up. Even at eight, she would often call me 'mud' or 'dum'...or perhaps they were Freudian slips?

However, one of her funniest muddle ups was when she was about five and we had been cycling in Richmond Park. She suddenly announced she was desperate for the loo. When told:

'You should have gone earlier, when I asked you before we started our ride. We're miles away from a loo now. You'll have to go behind that tree over there'

She replied:

'I can't possibly do that Mummy. Someone might see my privacy!'

We all thought that very funny and it's been inscribed on my memory ever since. She has always had a very good vocabulary but sometimes did not use words in their correct context. Written work was a jumbled muddle.. Her reading was not fluent. She just couldn't remember new words very easily. Then spelling them became an even bigger challenge. I would sit very patiently with her, prompting and encouraging her.her along, Attempting to find an easier way for her to both memorise and decode the words. Deespiteexp telling her, for example b-e-c-a-u-s-e was 'because', if she came across that same word only three lines later, she simply would not remember it at all. We had to constantly go over words repeatedly, reinforcing them by various means, whether it be a chalkboard, writing in sand or even icing the word on a cake. The food reinforcements seemed to work well! For remembering spellings, once she actually could recognise the word, mnemonics helped. i.e. **Because = big elephants can't add up sums easily**. As a visual learner, if Amelia could get a picture in her mind it would make all the difference.

In some ways, it was fortunate that there was a history of dyslexia difficulties in the family. Her dad, Graham, had to have a year at boarding school to have any chance of any O–levels. He achieved three despite predictions to the contrary. Auntie Lorraine had even greater difficulties. Although she had attended a private school from the age of nine, she became so school phobic that instead of going to school,she hid in the garden shed. Uncle Mike was the exception. He had no such difficulty. In fact he was very academic, gaining a place at a prestigious grammar school. Lorraine would bribe Mike to write absence notes for her!

Initially we couldn't see that Amelia would be academic in any way. At eight, she was already two years behind on her reading. She was on the special needs register from her first year at Infants. Unfortunately placing her on the table of dyslexic 'naughty and bullying boys', did little to help eother her education or self confidemce. Despite wanting to succeed, nothing on the page ever made any sesnse to herr. The boys were a distraction and a TA between six kids was not enough help. I decided to get an Educational Psychologist report to clearly establish that she was dyslexic and what help I could get the school to provide, or provide myself. As I had always suspected, she was dyslexic with the IQ test showing that Amelia was above average intelligence. Whether it was coincidence or not, it seemed to trigger a response at her school. Their SENCO had just left and as a replacement, they employed an excellent dyslexia specialist teacher. Mrs Fry was Amelia's very own Mary Poppins, working magic with her one to one support, amazing strategies and the wonderful after school SEN club. Despite the SEN club being on a Friday, it was so popular that all the non-SEN kids wanted to join in.

At about the same time, I was made redundant from P&O Business Travel. I've always clung to the belief that 'out of every adversity comes an opportunity' and I used my enforced break from travel to explore other opportunities. I had been an inactive member of the Medway Dyslexia Association for a couple of years, with Amelia still on their waiting list for Saturday morning lessons. I was aware that they ran a number of courses. By luck, or fate, they were running 'An Introduction to Supporting the Dyslexic Learner'. I signed up for the course but again by a twist of fate, ended up becoming their part-time administrator, which then led on to managing the centre and being very much involved in the world of dyslexia. I learnt a lot from manning the helpline, helping to organise conferences and typing up the assessment reports. 10% of the population, 4% severely so. However, by identifying the problem early and then putting in the necessary teaching and strategies, it can make a BIG difference. The difference between academic failure or success.

Because of the need for educating the educators and teaching those with dyslexic difficulties, we had various projects and contracts, including both the probation and prison service. It comes as no surprise as there is a link between offending and poor literacy skills. However, it's not lack of intelligence in most cases, just the inability to fully grasp the complexities of our written language. Many dyslexics are verbally erudite ...just don't ask them to get it down on paper!

It also helped me to help Amelia. Although dyslexia is not 'curable', strategies can help to mitigate its effects. Many 'aides memoires'. Post it notes are invaluable, devices for recording, a lap top computer and mind maps. Overlearning seems essential to really lodge information into the long-term memory. Encouragement also goes a long way. I've tried to instil a 'you can do

it' attitude.

After six years with the Medway Dyslexia Association, it became apparent that funding was becoming an issue. That's a lot of money to have to replace. Premises and staff are a very costly business and you need a considerable amount of money to keep it all going we had had an income of over 100K... We cut our overheads to the bare minimum, with only part-time working and the option to move to cheaper premises. We had also applied for a Lottery grant for another project with Medway Council. We had just finished a Children's Fund five year project. Sadly, despite getting through to the second round of the Lottery Funding hurdles, the funding should we receive it, was not going to arrive in time. With great sadness, after several meetings and an Emergency General Meeting, we had to wind up the Medway Dyslexia Association.

However, we had a wealth of expertise and enthusiasm, so Anne Powell (a former committee member of the MDA) made it her mission to set up a website and so Dyslexia House, like that hackneyed phoenix, rose from the ashes of the Medway Dyslexia Association.

I have now been Chair of Dyslexia House for more than five years. I will have to step down this year but will continue to be a committee member of the association. I have had great joy through my dyslexia world. I have made many new friends – Julie Sweeting, Anne and Peter Powell, Penny and Dario Modena, Pauline Bridges, Anne and John Sears, Di and Dave Maxwell, Joyce Wilford. Most important of all, I renewed a friendship with an old school friend, Liz.

Elizabeth Malyon, as I knew her at school, was involved in the drama productions as stage manager. Our love of theatre drew us together. Liz was a year older, leaving school to study Stage Management.

We lost touch after school, only to be reunited on Chessington North's railway platform in the 1980s. We became commuter buddies.

Gossiping about old school days on our commute to work. We lost touch when she moved to Scotland. It was a big surprise, therefore, to find our paths crossed again at the Medway Dyslexia Association. She was the Business Manager, when I went to help them out for three weeks, in exchange for that initial course I mentioned earlier. It really has been serendipity or fate working at its best. We spent six months as colleagues. The three week administration job became permanent. Liz, ever ambitious, then moved to the British Dyslexia Association as Regional Manager for Kent. The MDA committee offered me Liz's job. It all turned out very well indeed. Liz and I have now become the best of friends over the last 17 years. In fact, we've been away to Ireland together, for a mutual friend's and colleague's 40th birthday, visited her when she lived in Poland and since my sister and her brother, died we have become surrogate siblings.

So finishing the story, where I started.

Amelia.

For her, although she has struggled over the years, she proves that good support coupled with persistence and hard work pay off. She has had a very positive outcome. Fortunately, by the time she left St Paul's primary school, she was only three months behind on her reading. I was rather worried that she wouldn't cope at secondary school. Particularly when the SENCO advised there would be NO support 'as there are girls coming into year seven, with only a reading age of seven!' However, I needn't have worried. Tolworth Girls' School had a fantastic 'superhead', with very dyslexia friendly teaching methods. As a result they had a good academic record.

Amelia really progressed well, each year achieving better than the last. With the exception of French. Despite my suggestion, the school would not let her drop the subject. She did well in her GCSEs, with 10 passes above C, and some As for good measure. She only just failed French with a D and was bitterly disappointed. We had spent considerable time and effort with French. A-Levels were even better – she achieved two As and a B. That was the requirement for the Speech & Language Therapy Degree at Reading.

Gravesham Community Hospital now employs her as a SALT. It hasn't been easy. She was extremely stressed in the first six months. She didn't give in though and with encouragement. She is also learning new strategies to deal with the demands of the job. I have no doubt that given just a little bit more time; she will be an excellent therapist. She has some great qualities, including patience and empathy. Not only that but she has developed a love of reading and writing. It might take her longer than a non-dyslexic person but they are now both a joyful experience for her. She particularly enjoys travelling the world, describing her experiences in travel journals (a girl after my own heart). She has set up a blog, has made some entries but with the demands of her job has not added as much to it as she would have liked. I hope that she will rectify that at the end of the month when she is off to Sri Lanka.

I would say that Amelia has been made by dyslexia. She has, in turn, provided me with a pathway into the realm of dyslexia.

A surprising joy.

For further information see:

www.medwaydys.org

www.bda-dyslexia.org

POSTSCRIPT NOVEMBER 2020

On Monday 23 November I received very sad news.

Dyslexia House Association's loyal treasurer, Penny Modena, had passed away. Anne Powell had already alerted me a couple of days before that Penny was in the Covid Critical Care ward at Medway Maritime. She had not been well for several months. In her weakened state this horrible virus had done its worst.

To say it is heartbreaking is an understatement. Not only does her family suffer a huge loss, but the wider community will miss her tremendously. Dario has been overwhelmed with offers of support from all quarters. English Martyrs Church where she was an active member. The English Martyrs Primary School, where she was a governor. The pupils and parents she taught.

Penny gave her time and energy to so many people. She was everybody's friend. She truly embodied 'Joie de Vivre'.

A TALE OF TWO DICKENS

It was February 2003.

I had just had the horrible but not, unexpected news. I no longer had a job.

The previous three months at P&O Business Travel I had been working on the redundancy selection process, knowing very well that my boss, the Operations Director, had probably selected me for redundancy too. This was after the company had already consolidated various offices in the London and South East region. My first few months at P&O had actually been the best of times but the downturn in business travel following the awful terror attack of 9/11 in 2001 had continued. Despite our best efforts, staff cuts were unavoidable. It had been the single most stressful experience of my working career to date. Definitely the season of Darkness for me, and for a great many people their winter of despair.

So what to do now?

My previous company, HRG, were going through the same process, shedding staff by the tipper truckload. Ralph, my husband, who still worked at HRG, was on tenterhooks wondering whether he might share the same fate as me. We would then both be jobless with little chance of employment in the industry we had worked in collectively for over 50 years.

If anything, I am a born optimist. 'Out of every adversity comes an opportunity' has been my adage for as long as I can remember. After my sad leaving do on Friday 7th February, I sailed forth on my enforced unemployment cruise.

On Monday 10th, it was down to the serious business of looking for a job.

Perhaps it was time I became a teacher. I had been trying to assist my dyslexic daughter, Amelia, with her reading and writing struggles. Perhaps I should become a dyslexia specialist teacher. I knew there were local courses, as I had been a member of the Medway Dyslexia Association for many years. In fact, Amelia was still on their waiting list for Saturday tuition. Grabbing the Yellow Pages, I found their details and eagerly dialled the number. Kate, their very helpful administrator, gave me excellent news. Their OCN course 'Supporting the Dyslexic Learner' had just started the previous Wednesday evening. She would check with the course leader if I could enrol and ring me back.

By Wednesday morning, I had had no response, so with some anxiety I called again. This time, a very harassed Anne Sears, the Chair of the Association, was at the other end of the line. I explained my mission and she replied, very apologetically:

'Oh I'm so sorry. Kate has gone on immediate leave of absence due to some serious family matters. It has left us all rather in a pickle. We're in the middle of arranging a conference and she was the lynchpin in all the arrangements. I am trying to help, Liz, our business manager to pick up the pieces but she only works part-time and there's so much still to do. Everything's on the computer and I'm not very computer savvy.'

I could sense the desperation in her voice, she sounded very near to tears. She was clearly floundering like a lost soul in the Hades of cyberspace.

'Is there anything I can do to help?' I offered.

By the end of the call, I placed the phone back in its cradle with a flourish, practically high-fiving myself. Not only had I arranged to start the course that evening but I'd arranged an appointment to see Anne and the Treasurer, Jenny, later that day. Depending on my credibility, they were open to the possibility of a barter arrangement. The course in exchange for three weeks' work. I was feeling very optimistic. A spring of hope was starting to bubble up from the unlikely depths of Chatham High Street.

To add to this rather fateful opportunity, I was stunned to find that the Association's Business Manager, Liz, was someone I had known at school. Not only that, but when I had lived in Chessington in the 80's I had reunited with this very same Liz at Chessington North railway station and we had become commuter buddies. Sadly, we lost touch after she later moved to Scotland and I mislaid her address.

'I don't believe it' I exclaimed 'Elizabeth Malyon! We meet again.How spooky! I thought you were in Scotland?' I had long ago mislaid her address. She looked at me askance for a few moments. Then registered who I was:

'Judith Stow! How bizarre that you're in Medway too. I relocated down here six months ago to run the Association. What a small world!'

We hugged in front of the two bemused committee members. Without hesitation, Anne and Jenny then asked:

'When can you start?'

'Now, if you'd like me too' I replied with childish enthusiasm.

This was to become my epoch of incredulity and my introduction to Rochester's Dickens' Festivals. My three-week stint at the MDA stretched to 'indefinite' as Kate the administrator then 'resigned for personal reasons'.

I continued to enjoy working alongside Liz on various projects but the looming one was the 'Summer Dickens'. We had to prepare a stall for dyslexia literature and information boards. To raise funds we also arranged for various diversions from a balloon race and a Tombola to eclectic handmade crafts. At home, I had my mum running up items on her sewing machine whilst I hand painted terracotta pots to fill with geraniums. Liz myself and some other volunteers even spent an evening round at Mum's house making things for the stall.

Excitement about the event gripped me. I spent weeks scouring the charity shops for suitable attire. I found a long black satin and lace evening dress that was just about acceptable. It was a bit clingy though. To iron out all my less than desirable bulges, a pair of control underwear was required. Or Bridget Jones' knickers, as I affectionately call them. When the July date of the festival arrived, it was the hottest day of that year so far. Not an ideal day to squeeze oneself into a heat absorbing long dress. Even in the shade of the stall's gazebo we were roasting like plump potatoes, unattractive blooms of sweat appearing under bosoms and armpits. Yet despite the intense heat, we were having fun on our stall in the shadow of Rochester Castle. It was a magical day with endless parades of Dickensian characters passing by. By early evening, packing everything up, we were no doubt suffering from heat exhaustion. Yet happy in the knowledge we had raised dyslexia awareness and quite a few hundred pounds in the process.

Ralph came to collect me and before we had even left the car park, I was struggling to remove the now very uncomfortable Bridget Jones' knickers. However, as I raised the skirt of the dress I was horrified.

'Ralph look at the tops of my thighs and legs!' We were both staring at a very unpleasant black blue mottled bruising. Shocked, we both tugged at the offending knickers, which seemed to have been cutting off my blood supply to cause such an effect.

'Are your legs numb?' Ralph, asked, genuinely worried.

'Well, funnily enough, no' I answered both bemused and anxious. 'But it's a huge relief to get those BJ's off. Perhaps a shower down and brisk rub will restore the circulation?'

We screeched out of Rochester, breaking the speed limit all the way to Cuxton. I was practically stripping off articles of clothing as I hurtled through the front door and straight up into the shower. It was such a relief to have the cooling water cascade over a very hot and bothered body. Then I noticed the blue/black liquid trickling down the drain. My legs were starting to look normal again, if with a little bit of a blue tinge.

'Ralph, Ralph! Come and look at this!' Ralph bolted up the stairs. We both started to laugh hysterically as dark blue rivulets flowed down my legs to the plughole.

'What a relief!' I gasped between paroxysms of laughter.

So much for my first introduction to Dickens' Festivals.

The 'Christmas Dickens' was the next big fundraising event on the calendar. Liz had organised a tremendously successful stall selling mulled wine and mince pies the previous year so with some trepidation I took on the challenge. For a week leading up to the festival our house resembled a wine depot. We could hardly get through the front door for the mountain of red wine boxes. It was suggested, in addition to the mulled wine and mince pies, we also have a Father Christmas and try to do seasonal photos of the younger children. This was an additional complication. A case of 'everything before us and nothing before us'. The promised outfit did not materialise resulting in frantic calls ringing around all of our contacts for a substitute. In the end, I had to borrow the local infants' school's costume, hot and steaming, straight from Santa at their Christmas Fair.

There was no let up the evening before the 'Christmas Dickens'. We were brewing up oranges and cinnamon sticks to an old Dickensian recipe...the secret ingredient for our 'Ye Olde Mulled Wine'. The whole house smelt incredibly festive for days after!

At dawn, on that freezing cold Saturday, we barely managed to get all the boxes and other paraphernalia into the car. Local estate agents' had kindly lent us their premises for the weekend so that we had access to storage, electricity and water. We unpacked, erected the gazebo at the front of the shop and got the mulled wine brewing. Not that we had many customers for the wine at 09.00. It was bitterly cold day, with outside temperatures barely above freezing. I was very pleased of the fake fur coat that I had on over my colourfast long black dress. The earlier offending dress long consigned to the rubbish bin. Though not all of the 24 volunteers had, come quite appropriately dressed for such cold weather. One young woman seemed to have come straight from the nightclub in a scanty outfit more suited to the 'Summer Dickens'. She spent very little time helping, instead retreating to the warmer haven of the back office. Luckily, our other stalwart volunteers, including Liz and my stepdaughter, Christine, were able to take up the slack.

The cold weather certainly had an effect on our mulled wine sales. By 10 O'clock, queues were forming for our over-generous cups of deliciously smelling liquid. Consequently, by the end of Saturday, we had a potential problem. I confided in my chief volunteer:

'Ralph, we're going to run out of mulled wine tomorrow. We only have one box left. I think you selected too large a cup when we bought the supplies!'

Ralph, ever confident, allayed my fears:

'Don't worry. I can nip down to Bookers, first thing in the morning. They're open at 08.00. That should give us just enough time to drop off the gear, erect the gazebo and get the wine back before the 09.00 start deadline'

We weren't expecting an additional panic. Whilst setting everything up, I had inadvertently locked ourselves out of the estate agents, with the car keys still in their offices. After a gut wrenching moment of dismay, we realised we could break in to the offices by dismantling their letterbox. I narrowly squeezed my hand through the letterbox opening to unscrew the loose nuts. Thank goodness no police were patrolling the High Street at that time to witness our felonious activities. We never did admit to our hosts about breaking and entering!

The rest of the day was thankfully calm and uneventful and, in the main part, fun. We returned home on Sunday evening, cold, hoarse, exhausted but strangely elated. We had survived the rigours of the 'Christmas Dickens'. We had enjoyed its old-fashioned ambience and in the process had sold over 2,000 glasses of mulled wine and almost as many mince pies. The profit going into the Medway Dyslexia Association's coffers was over £1,000. It was a success!

Whether it was the best of times or the worst of times, it's still difficult to tell. There were certainly elements of both. Yet without doubt my experience of the Two Dickens' Festivals, was not only memorable but character building.

I think Charles would have approved!

Liz at the desk whch was to become mine within a few months

THE JOY OF BEING BLONDE

August 2010

On one August bank holiday Sunday my in-laws were at our house. In the late afternoon we had an unexpected visitor. My husband opened the door and found a tall blue-uniformed figure on our doorstep. He asked if my husband was the registered owner of the grey Zafira parked outside. They had CCTV footage from a local garage after an incident of someone driving away without paying for their FULL tank petrol. The very charming and attractive young policeman (PC Jones – I have his mobile number!) explained:

'The person in question was a blonde lady with a pony tail.'

He was diplomatic enough to not mention 'middle-aged'. He waved a CD – the evidence of my misdeed, which of course my husband insisted on seeing. We trooped upstairs to the study to view the offending item on the computer. Yes, it was undoubtedly me clearly replacing the nozzle, purposefully screwing the petrol cap back on and then nimbly hopping back into the car and driving off. I giggled; a hot flush of embarrassment coursing through my body. I had no recollection of not paying ...such is the danger of both being a blonde and entering the Saga years. My in-laws found it very entertaining and have been dining out on the story ever since. I of course took full mileage too with my final throw-away line before our visitor left:

'The things I do to get the attention of a man in uniform! '

PC Jones was very sweet and said it happens quite a lot. I noticed he even visited in an unmarked police car to save embarrassment!

I will now have to sheepishly tell my old school friends about my blonde moment. The previous March I gave my friend Anne (a teacher) a hard time over her 'oversight'- walking off without paying for an item.

However, my blonde moment definitely eclipses Anne's Saga moment!

Oh the joy of being blonde.

THE JOY OF ILS

Summer 2013

The ILs are my lovely in-laws. In their late eighties they were struggling to lead independent lives. MIL had been diagnosed with dementia in her early eighties. Unable to do even the basic household chores....or at least that's what she says.....so FIL took over all the household jobs and became her full time carer.

FIL had always been very active and sprightly despite living with a pace maker for more than twenty five years and prostate cancer for at least seven years. A six monthly anti-cancer injection, he philosophically stated: "keeps me alive".

In 2012 looking after their fairly large garden seemed to be taking its toll. The greenhouse, usually crammed with luscious tomato plants, stunningly sunny marigolds and pillar box red geraniums, was abandoned to the weeds. The normally neat lawn and flowerbeds started to look neglected. The Secret Gardener offered to take over that job. However, as much as they enjoy looking out of the window at their garden, they would rather have a social with me (the Secret Gardener).

So between sessions of frantic activity in the garden, I wiped the sweat from my brow, the mud from my hands, made us all cups of tea and sat down for a chat.

As a result I have learnt all sorts of things about my ILs. Many aspects of their lives that even my husband had no idea about. The following snippets I intend to keep for the rest of the family as part of their family history. I sorely regret not having done this more thoroughly with my own mum (or dad for that matter). I did encourage my mum to write down her recollections on the lap top I gave her. She had been an excellent typist all her working life and even trained others on the early word processors. However, age and new technology defeated her. I even bought her a Dictaphone that worked with Dragon, a software to convert speech into text. That didn't work either. She managed the first ten pages or so of her memoirs but after that it all came to a halt. I now realise that I should have just sat down with her once a week and coaxed the memories from her, typing them as we talked. I am determined that I shall not let the opportunity pass with my ILs.

We started with FIL, as he is chattier and very keen to tell me about his early life and war experiences. MIL is more of a challenge as she tends to drift off into her own little world and it's more difficult to coax the memories from the confused recesses of her brain.

FIL'S recollections

"I was born on 11 July 1925 in Willow Walk which was part of the Kentish Town Fire Station. In those days that's where we lived. Every Fire Station had accommodation for firemen and their families. I was lucky enough to go to the new Arnos School in Arnos Grove (Palmers Green) when it opened in 1938. I remember singing in the choir at the opening ceremony. Although I enjoyed school, I wasn't particularly academic. My favourite subjects were art, history and geography. I was rubbish at English and literature despite enjoying reading.

I left school just as the war started. At 14 I was far too young for the army. I managed to get myself a job as a warehouseman in the stores in GK in Edmonton.

However, I often got dirty looks from the girls at work as they thought every young man should be in the army. I was fairly tall for my age and did not like to be the object of their disdain. However, there was not much I could do about it. I just had to wait until I was old enough to enlist.

I hadn't been working that long when Dad changed Fire Stations and we relocated to Worcester Park in Surrey. It was for two reasons. Firstly, for safety of the family and secondly to be near the company that manufactured equipment used by the London Fire Brigade. Sieby Gorman was moving from its' central London location in Westminster Bridge Road to the safer haven of Chessington. My dad had a lot of dealings with this company as they manufactured the breathing apparatus that Dad had to train his colleagues to use. Another reason for moving to Worcester Park was so that I could start work at Siebe Gorman. Dad had got to know the owner, Sir Robert Davis, and pulled a few strings to get me an apprenticeship.

We no longer lived at the Fire Station then but moved into a fairly newly built bungalow at 12 The Warren. A lovely spacious place, overlooking a neat green square. It was quite different from Arnos Grove (Palmers Green, North London). Worcester Park was a very countrified place back in the 40's, with pheasants regular visitors to our garden.

I remember being on permanent night duties at Siebe Gorman. From 7pm-7am. Most people cycled everywhere, so I naturally had to cycle to work. Cars were only for the wealthy. We had to be very careful with our bikes. They were precious. There was so much shrapnel on the road that it could easily slice your tyres. We had to make do and mend everything. I clearly remember having to repair my cycle battery on more than one occasion, as well as constantly patching punctured tyres.

My route from Worcester Park to Chessington took me around the Tolworth roundabout, past the large and well frequented Toby Jug pub."

This part of FIL's history is particularly interesting to me. I lived in Chessington for 15 years and still visit the area on a regular basis, as my kids, Greg and Amelia still live there. Sadly the area has not improved for the better. The Toby Jug is now an unsightly Bowling Alley complex. Overshadowing the large roundabout is the hideous Tolworth Tower. A 60's grey concrete tower block that has nothing to recommend it. I tell FIL he won't be impressed with the changes with Tolworth.

Although Worcester Park is still very pleasant and The Warren is still very much as it was then. The bungalow he lived in is still there but if he wanted to move back to his childhood home it would probably cost in the region of £500,000. Parts of Worcester Park are incredibly expensive now. I promise to take him back there when his back is up to the journey. He continues the description of his teenage life:

"I remember going in the Toby Jug regularly. However one time I went in there with Maureen, my girlfriend at the time. She was an Irish girl....I can't stand the Irish now. Someone doctored my drink and I went to work drunk. One of my colleagues stuck me in the toilet until I sobered up. If the bosses had found out I was drunk, I would have been fired on the spot. It taught me a lesson. I never went drinking before I went to work again. We did get a break for lunch but our lunchtime was 1am in the morning. We would eat in the canteen and then take a brief stroll down the road to see the anti-aircraft guns and searchlights.

The factory girls were particularly keen to go, so that they could chat up the soldiers. Quite often everybody would end up singing with the soldiers. All the modern songs of the day....Vera Lynn, Bing Crosby, Frank Sinatra".

I know FIL loves music, particularly military band music and I ask if he played an instrument.

"No, my love of brass bands come from listening to the Fire Brigade

Band which Dad played in. He played piccolo, oboe and clarinet. Though I did enjoy the popular dance bands of the day – Tommy Dorsey, Benny Goodman and the like. "

We resume FIL's story of his apprentice years:

"On the way back to the factory, I would pass the rubber factory on Jubilee Way. There was always a very pungent aroma. We jokingly called it the Durex factory! I clearly remember my cycle home after finishing my night shift at 7am. More often than not there would be a large owl perched on a post not far from my home. He would stare at me with his huge amber eyes. Occasionally I would get a hoot as well. It was a very welcome sight.

Sieby Gorman, my employer, specialized in marine engineering before the war but during the war it manufactured a whole array of equipment for the war effort: diving bells, diving suits, breathing apparatus, safety lamps for miners plus lots of other highly technical parts and equipment. Even torpedo parts. However, there was quite a lot of secrecy just in case there were any spies infiltrating the factory.

The factory had a glass roof which the staff were rather concerned about because if we were bombed we would be cut to shreds. However, we were told not to worry as the roof had been painted to look like a farm! We never were bombed, so the farm ruse must have worked.

I remember thinking that it looked like a fairyland of lights when the Incendiaries were dropped. They fell from the sky in bread baskets. Despite the devastation they caused, they did look very pretty on their descent. I remember one particular day, I think it must have been a Sunday, as my dad was about. During the week we didn't see much of him as he was always so busy. Although at least he was at home and not a soldier. As a fireman he was not called up. He was in one of the "reserved occupations". Yes, this one particular Sunday we were blitzed with incendiaries. We had to try putting out the fires when they landed. Some were exploding and looked like huge fireworks. Fires were erupting here and there in The Warren. There was a bucket outside each house, in case of incendiaries. However, people hadn't been keeping them topped up and we found that most of them were empty.

Dad and I were racing to fill up buckets and extinguish the fires. Everyone must have fled to the safety of their Morrison shelters. It was lucky that Dad and I were around to put out the fires, otherwise there would have been a lot more damage. I don't remember being frightened at the time, as we were just too busy.

As soon as I could, I volunteered for the army at 18.

I didn't keep a diary until towards the end of the war as we were told not to. However, Dad said I should keep some record, so I took his advice rather than the official line. I had to keep it well out of sight, otherwise it would have been confiscated."

I have seen these diaries and although not very detailed, it does give an insight into FIL's daily life. However, the following recollections are without the aid of the diaries. Just vivid memories.

Overloon, Holland – September 1944

"There were two recollections I had from this time:

We were ensconced in deep trenches below ground. The Germans didn't know we were there and we wanted to keep it that way. Our trench was right on the edge of the area. There were always drainage ditches.

It was at dawn and I was on guard duty. There in the drainage ditches I could see Germans crawling along the ditch. I raised the alarm and the whole Platoon scrambled to attention, rifles raised ready to blast the Germans when they reached the end of the ditch. Imagine my mortification when the "Germans" actually emerged from the ditch. They weren't Germans at all, but pigs. Their muddy backs looked like camouflage battle dress. To say my name was mud is an understatement. I should have gone to Supersavers! We couldn't even shoot the pigs in order to have bacon for breakfast as we didn't want to draw attention to our hidden trenches. This was a rather bizarre situation.

There were four Germans soldiers guarding a farm building during the day and then would retreat at night. We would take up their positions during the night. Then we would pull back during the day and the Germans would take up our positions. However, they were friendly Krauts – they would leave us messages asking if we had cigarettes and if we left them cigarettes they would leave us bottles of Schnapps.

The Germans got into trouble for leaving the Schnapps and taking the cigarettes, as they were within viewing distance we could see the German officer bawling at them for their misdemeanors.

Gun, Holland – Christmas 1944

As the Kings Own Scottish Borders Regiment wanted New Year's Day off, we had Christmas Day off and covered for them at New Year.

I remember that Christmas Day very clearly. We went to the chapel. It was absolutely packed full to the rafters, but the Dutch locals had saved spaces between them for us to join their families to make up the family party. They sang the carols in Dutch & we sang in English. The next day the locals provided a variety show for us but as it was all in Dutch, they had to do charades to convey the meaning. They offered us accommodation in their apple lofts on the farms, so that we didn't have to sleep in the trenches but it was so cold the blankets froze and we had to stand them against the wall to thaw out.

Helmond – 1944

I certainly remember the winter in Helmond. It was very harsh and snowy. Where we were was not the flat terrain you associate with Holland – this was the hilly bit near Maastricht.

We were billeted at 33 Bunzig Straat and the school was the HQ for 3rd Division of the 21st Army Group. 2nd Battalion Royal Ulster Rifles. There were 3 billeted. It was a tiny house – couldn't have held more. We were all in one room – the loft. Literally three beds. Luckily we had water bottles (not the drinking type) as it was miles from the privy....probably outside but never used it. We had to hang on to our number two's until we were back at the school.

I remember the Dutch youngsters being intimidated by us. Not surprising after the presence of the Germans. They used to scatter when they saw us coming. However, the two girls in the house, Lena and Truus were more approachable. There was a curfew on but despite that, we took the youngsters to the NAAFI and the soldiers on guard duty just turned a blind eye. The girls were the link between us and the local community. After one particularly heavy fall of snow they encouraged the children to pelt us with snowballs. After that jolly good snowball fight, the kids were no longer intimidated by us. Yes, I certainly remember that snowy period and having to trudge back to our billets, the crisp new snow squeaking under our heavy army boots.

We felt sorry for the family we were billeted with, as we didn't really have anything to offer them. Occasionally we would manage to swipe a tin of corned beef from the provisions in the school. We would hand it over to the granddad of the family. However, we then realized that the granddad was selling the corned beef at the back door and making a fortune on the black market with it!

***River Isis 1945** –*

The attack went without any problems at all. The mine clearance people came to check for mines. There were a huge amount of box mines. The Germans thought that we would not be able to advance because of the mines. However, the clearance people found that the mines had become waterlogged and inoperative, thus making our attack a doddle.

They told us to remove the 4-second grenades and replace them with 10-second ones. You unscrew the cap, remove the fuse and swap them round. However one of our comrades removed the pin without unscrewing the cap and taking out the fuse. When he realized his mistake he shouted "It's live!" We all threw ourselves out of the window. It was just as well the window was already blown out, as we would have been in trouble.

There was also the time we worked with the secret service – MI6. That was in the Rhineland. The River Maas was at the back of us and the Rhine in front of us. We had been right up against the flood banks of the Rhine, which were quite a lot taller than the farmhouse we were in. We were called out as we had to form a team. We had to practice at night going down the flood banks of the Rhine and going down the other side. We did this for a few nights then they presented us with a canoe and we had to practice getting that up and down the banks too. Then this mysterious character turned up and we had to get the canoe up the bank and down again for him to paddle across the Rhine. However he was only gone minutes. We were watching him but he about turned and came paddling back. The canoe had a hole in it so that mission was abandoned.

We never did know what that was all about.

Bremen - the end of the war

When it was announced that the war was finally over, the German officer, whose house we took over, came out with a tray full of drinks and asked us to 'Keep it clean,' wishing us all the best.

He was from the mounted artillery division but had a wooden leg! He was a smart, upright fellow in riding britches, carrying a sword. After the brutality of the war, this was all very surreal and incredibly civilized.

To crown it all I was in the casualty clearing centre. There was huge relief and jubilation to know the war was over. The thing which I found very amusing, was that, rather coincidentally, most of the bed cases who had been injured and were seemingly unable to return to the front line, made a remarkable instant recovery. The day before they were unable to move and now they were on their feet eager to get back home. Such is the miraculous effect of that piece of joyous news!"

MIL during FIL's chatty recollections drifts off into her own little world. Although MIL did not play an active part in the drama of war, I want her recollections too.

MIL'S recollections

I was born at 83 Brownlow Road, New Southgate N13 on 1st March 1926. They were quite big houses, divided into flats.

My mum, Antoinette, came over from Holland in 1919 to work in the upholstery business. Her maiden name was Van Os. She was really escaping her family and friends who had shunned her for going out with a protestant. They were strict Catholics and very Victorian in their views. Mum met Dad through work, as he was also an upholsterer. Ironically Mum's parents never knew that Dad was NOT a Catholic. Or at least not until Dad died. Mum and Dad went to a protestant High Church, which operated very much like a Catholic church. Even when Tante Joanna came over, she didn't rumble the deception, although to be fair, she was a bit simple.

We later moved to 110 Fairway New Southgate. It was a lovely spacious double fronted house. My youngest sister, Cynthia, was born at that house. So I guess I must have been about three or four years old. It was a brand new council house with a long garden. Dad had the bottom half to grow vegetables and potatoes. I remember Dad doing a lot of gardening and he also had an allotment very close to the house. Dad (Edward) took me to Barrowell Green open air swimming pool. Broomfield Park was another local park we enjoyed visiting.

I went to Oakwood School in Southgate. It was a brand new school when I went there. I was very sporty and ran for the school. I was also in the netball team.

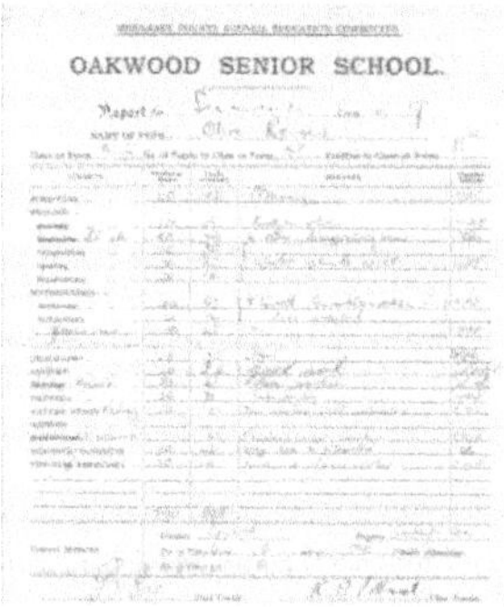

OAKWOOD SENIOR SCHOOL.

I remember my dad taking me to school as he was out of work for some time. My mum was busy with my younger sisters. Dad had been a master upholsterer by trade and even did work for the royalty. During the depression of 1926 he lost his job and ended up taking a job at the mental hospital in Friern Barnet. He taught the inmates how to upholster, presumably as part of their rehabilitation into normal life and probably providing some revenue for the hospital. He had interests outside of his job, he was a great reader and even volunteered in the library at Oakwood School, which was open some evenings. He was also an active member of the Labour Party. We never had a TV when my dad was alive but we had a very nice radio.

Christmases as a child were wonderful. They were spent with our paternal grandparents in Southgate. Granddad Reeves outlived Grandma Reeves. He ended up living with one of my aunties, Lalle, so we went to her house then at Christmas time and then cousin Daphne came down from Croydon. Her parents were Auntie Lou and Uncle Reg, Peter and Pam, dad's eldest sister). Auntie Connie was Dad's youngest sister. He had just the three sisters. Pam was a cousin.'

MIL's cousin Jeanette has also provided some missing details.

Jeanette's recollections

'Our aunts were Irene, Louisa, Connie and Alice. Lallie was my mum. and Connie. John was the brother. He was a bit simple. My Mother looked after her parents in the family home, where my sisters and I were born, 122 Stanley Road, New Southgate.

I think it was my sister, Mary who would speak to Olive at No.29 Brownlow Road as I did too

In the last ten years, Ron and I would chat away as Olive was usually in bed!

I always had a soft spot for Ron. I loved his mischievous sense of humour. Being 11 years younger than Olive some details I don't know or remember but over the last 25 years or so our ages seem to have got closer and we have enjoyed many happy days together.

Sadly Mary had a severe stroke in September 2015 and was no longer able to communicate, but was cared for in a residential home in Ipswich. She died in September 2017. I have always been quite humbled when Olive asked my Dad, her Uncle Albert to 'give her away' at her wedding.'

MIL continues:

'Oh yes, I remember we also spent weekends with Auntie Rene and Uncle George, Daphne, Peter and Pam in Croydon. Uncle George, Daphne's dad was a butcher and they lived opposite the butcher's shop. I remember having the most delicious juicy joints of meat to eat at their house. Daphne was an only child for a long time. She was the same age as me.

Before the war we had some lovely holidays in Holland, as half of my cousins were Dutch. My mum was born in Holland. They came from The Hague. They lived near Schrevingen. It was within walking distance of the beach, although quite a hike though. I remember that lovely sandy beach with dunes in the background. The tide would go out for miles.

We went with mum and my sisters for most of the summer, then dad followed on later for a couple of weeks. I remember those long balmy summer days. It was idyllic. Just perfect! What fun we had with our cousins, Rie and Darm, who spoke excellent English. Cousin Louis was much the same age as Pat, so on holidays they gravitated towards each other. However, no romance blossomed. When another cousin asked Pat:

'Don't you find him handsome?'

Pat retorted:

'No, he's far too pretty!'

Their mum (Tante Mien) and dad (Uncle Omioop) were very kind to us. Uncle Omioop was an English teacher, so his English was excellent. They came over to visit several times. They were quite well off and popped in to see us on their way to Southampton to go on cruises.

We were thoroughly spoilt by our Grandmother (Oma) Maria Alida Titulair and Grandfather (Opa) Daniel Van Os. My grandparents were well off. It was a large two story house with a loft room. It had 4 bedrooms. We managed to fit in quite comfortably. Sadly I can't remember what grandfather (Opa) did for a job. There were quite a few Aunties, Uncles and other cousins who thoroughly spoilt us. They were wonderful times but now sadly just hazy memories. I do remember eating a lot of fresh fish, which is probably why my favourite meal is fish and chips.

Sadly all of the Dutch family of my generation are gone. Grandad Van Os died 6th March 1955. We were on holiday in Jaywick (Clacton). We came home to find a telegram but we were too late for the funeral.

I wrote to Rie (Rite) for many years and carried on visiting her. She died in 2004.

The only family members of my generation still alive today are my sister Pat. I keep in contact with my cousin Jeannette (her Mum was Dad's sister). Jeannette was the youngest of three. Cath was one of them who I speak to occasionally. She continued to live in Palmers Green, North London but now lives in Norwich.

It's a pity that connections have been lost to the Van Os side of the family. Just doing a google search for Van Os near The Hague and this interesting titbit of information popped up. It would be lovely to think that MIL is connected to this artistic strand of Van Os':

From Wikipedia, the free encyclopedia

Pieter Gerardus van Os *(8 October 1776 – 28 March 1839) was a Dutch painter and engraver and a member of the renowned Van Os family of artists.Van Os was born in The Hague the son of Jan van Os. He studied with his father and from 1794 to 1795 at the Tekenakademie in The Hague.*

Died From Injuries

Tragic Death Of Labour Party Offical

Mr. Edward Charles Reeves, aged 44, of 110 Fairway, Southgate, died in the North Middlesex County Hospital on Monday from multiple injuries sustained in an accident at Cockfosters on Saturday morning.

We understand that Mr. Reeves was passenger in the side-car of a motor-cycle combination travelling north at about 6.30 a.m., and that it was foggy at the time.

There was a collision in the main road in which the combination, a bus and lorries were involved. The driver of the motor-cycle was not injured, but Mr. Reeves was hurried by Southgate Ambulance to the North Middlesex Hospital.

An inquiry into the circumstances will be held on Friday morning at 10 o'clock in the hospital.

MUCH-LIKED MAN.

Mr. Reeves was a very much appreciated official of the Southgate Labour Party, first in the South Ward.

For the past ten years, however, his considerable energies had been concentrated upon the Party's work in the North West Ward of which, at the time of his death, he was hon. secretary, succeeding Mr. H. D. Dinmore, who regretfully had to resign the position.

He had been M.C. of their whist drives for seven years, and was highly esteemed by borrowers for his voluntary work at at the County Library branch in Oakwood School.

Said Mr. Dinmore to the "Gazette"—"He was a fine man, energetic, always one of the workers, and we shall all miss him immensely."

We understand that he was an upholsterer by trade and that he leaves a wife and three young children, all girls.

Whilst my dad was working my mum was a full-time housewife. Dad sadly was killed in a road accident when I was just twelve so he wasn't around for the war. Les was a friend and work colleague in the same hospital where dad worked. He had motorbike with a side car and gave him a lift to work. That particular day it was very foggy and a lorry tried to overtake a bus. A bus went in to the sidecar. Dad didn't have a chance. I didn't go to my dad's funeral. My sisters and I went to my auntie's as I guess we were considered too young to attend the funeral. We were all devastated when dad died. Our lives changed totally.

I was thirteen when the war began and wasn't evacuated during the war. However, with advent of war, many schools had to be closed due to their lack of shelters.

Sequel To Fatal Accident

BUS DRIVER SUMMONED

Collision With Motor Cycle Combination

The driver of a bus which was involved in a collision with a motor cycle combination in the fog on the morning of March 5th, as a result of which a passenger received fatal injuries, appeared at Enfield Police Court on Monday summoned for driving in a dangerous manner and without due care and attention.

The passenger in the sidecar was a well-known member of Southgate Labour Party, Mr. Edward Charles Reeves, aged 41, a journeyman upholsterer, who lived at 110 Fairway, Southgate, and who died in the County Hospital, Edmonton, two days after the accident.

Defendant, Robert James Gibbs, Whitehouse Avenue, Boreham Wood, pleaded not guilty to both summonses.

The driver of the motor cycle combination, Leslie William Russell, of East Pole Cottages, Bramley Road, Southgate, said he was proceeding along Cockfosters Road in the direction of Potters Bar. It was very foggy at the time and visibility was only 10 yards. He was driving at 10-15 m.p.h. close to his nearside kerb when "suddenly, out of the fog a bus appeared straight in front of me, right on my side of the road. I saw that if I stopped on my right side there would be a head-on collision. I swerved to the right, but the sidecar just caught the nearside wheel of the bus.

"My combination was twisted right round in the road and an oncoming lorry just touched the bike, making a slight dent on the tank. The sidecar was completely smashed and my friend received bad internal injuries from which he did not recover."

Witness said he considered the bus was going fairly fast considering the visibility.

HOW BUS OVERTOOK LORRY.

Walter William Giddings, 38 Marshalls Avenue, St. Albans, said he was driving a lorry towards Southgate, following another lorry drawing a trailer. His speed was 8-10 m.p.h. He heard a hooter sounded about three times. Then a bus passed him at a speed of about 14-15 m.p.h. The bus was accelerating. The next thing he saw was a motor cycle and sidecar strike the bus. He did not think the bus had slackened speed.

He added that the fog was very thick, and in cross-examination said he did not see the driver of the leading lorry give a signal when the bus driver hooted. As he was driving so close to the lorry he was not in a good position to see if the driver did give a signal.

Russell Thomas Trethewie, of Southgate Road, Potters Bar, said he was following the bus, which was only just moving at the time of the impact.

P.C. Shinn said visibility where the accident occurred was 10-15 yards.

STATEMENT TO POLICE.

Insp. Kelly said defendant made the following statement, "The brick lorry gave me the right of way. He was doing about 3 m.p.h. I was passing him when I saw a motor cycle combination was coming from Barnet. I sounded my horn five times. He tried to swerve to the offside, but caught my nearside front wheel and then the side of the bus."

On this evidence the hearing was adjourned for a week for the attendance of another witness.

Fortunately our school didn't close.

It was hard work for her bringing us three girls up. Mum had to find a job to support us and ended up working in the Metal Box factory. She was working on a production line. So we were used to being on our own; Mum and the three girls. She worked very hard to support us and did her very best to keep us happy.

Then, not only having lost Dad, the war changed everything again. It was very hard for my mum (Antoinette) as she had no relatives close by to help out. During those awful days of the war, we had an Anderson shelter in the garden at home although we didn't use it. Mum was an air raid warden. So whenever there was an alarm she would normally have to get to work leaving us girls alone. We didn't like the idea of going into the Anderson shelter, so we stayed put in the house.

So during the war we just tried to find somewhere safe to be in the house. Normally in the front room but we didn't even get under the table when bombs were dropping and exploding close by. I remember once I just came downstairs from using the toilet. I had been thinking about having a bath but decided not to. It was just as well, as the window was blown in that night!

Pat is three years younger than me and Cynthia was only 14 months younger than Pat. Although we girls were very close, we didn't have the same friendship groups.

When it was announced that the war was over there was a huge sense of relief – it was wonderful. We, like most of Great Britain, had a street party. There was much dancing, singing and celebrating.

However, I met Ron through Pat. Ron knew one of Pat's friends, Margaret. Originally Ron was going out with Pat but I stole him away! We didn't fall out over it. Ron said he preferred blondes! Pat was dark.

My last address before Ron and I married was 56 Hawthorne Ave, Palmers Green. My mum bought that house from some friends. It was in a terrace of four. There was an alleyway to get to the back garden. It was a three bedroomed house with a lounge and dining room. Ron and I moved in with my mother in law and Ron's auntie Diddy once we were married. That was at 288 North Circular Road, Palmers Green. It was a three bedroomed house but the rooms were large. My mother in law worked from home on a huge loom (in the lounge). She made military badges, some embroidered with real silver or gold thread. She would stencil the outline of the badge onto the cloth which was stretched between the loom.

Diddy worked locally in a department store (Evans & Davis) in Palmers Green.

We were just 23 when we married on 26 March 1949. Ron had his 23rd birthday the previous July and I had just had my birthday on 1st March. I remember standing on the steps of the church, Christchurch Southgate, and whilst posing for the pictures we were distracted by the hockey being played on the green in front of the church. We were always interested in sports.

We had a week's honeymoon at the Claremont Private Hotel in St Michael's Road, Bournemouth. It cost £10 13 shillings and sixpence….we still have the receipt! We had our reception at home as couldn't afford to do anything else. It was a struggle to pay for the food and drinks for the wedding guests…but my mum's brother, Tom, realized that what we had provided would not be enough for all the guests so he just went out and got more drink and plonked it on the table. There weren't enough chairs to go around either and people had to sit on the stairs.

Although we never had any money spare after our food and fares to work, they were happy times, full of promise.

Even when Ralph and Hugh were born, we still lived in that house, but at some point when the boys were very small we moved in with my Mum in Hawthorne Avenue. Mum had the lounge as her bedroom. We all lived there together until 1967 when Ron was asked by Burroughs Wellcome to relocate to Dartford. I started work at 14. I was taught shorthand and typing but preferred figure work. So went more into the accounts side. I worked in the Sales Department for Burroughs Wellcome. I met Joan there. We became firm friends and are still friends today.

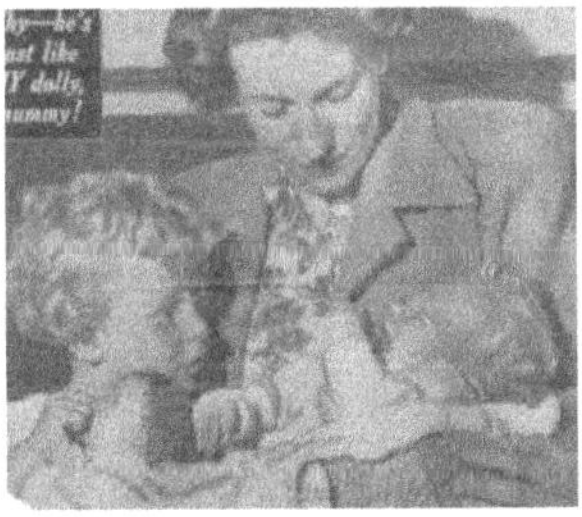

I think this is a photo of Joan with Ernest and Christine

Joan at the ripe age of 94

The job was in the head office in Euston Road. Living in North London it was an easy journey to work on the tube. I was there for 10 years. Happy times but decided to give Ron a chance of a job as he had been de-mobbed and hadn't any particular skills. So in 1950 Ron took over my job at the Overseas Division, Export Services Department. Nobby Clark was the Shipping Manager and most people were frightened of him. I wasn't though and Ron wasn't going to be frightened of him either .The change was as good as a rest. I went to a different company Lone Star which was local. Just opposite the Town Hall in Palmers Green. It was a toy manufacturer. I worked in the office on the accounts side. I gave up work in 1954, when Ralph came along.

Sometime before Hugh was born we moved to my mum's house in Hawthorn Avenue and then Hugh followed on in November, 1959, after a five year gap. Then I worked for Haringey Stadium in their office working out the bets. I was there on the greyhound racing nights on Mondays and Tuesdays. As a result I got free tickets to the stock-car racing, so that Ron could take Ralph. We moved from North London to New Eltham. I then became a civil servant working for the Tax Office in. I was there until I retired, which was after Ron. I carried on working until 60.

During the time the children were growing up, we did some homeworking. We painted plastic animals for a toy company called Brittons or Tempo. It didn't pay much, you had to paint a lot of them to make a pound. It was something that all the family could do together, so it was fun. It went towards the family holidays."

Ralph has a slightly different angle on that story. He remembers his Nan and Auntie coming round to dinner but they would have to paint the figures first. Not so much singing for your supper, definitely a case of painting for your supper.

FIL at this stage interjects with one of his Burroughs Wellcome stories:

"I was in charge of the credit notes. The Beckenham location were breeding guinea pigs and rats for sale to other companies. One of our customers in Sweden rang to tell us the animals had not arrived alive. I was asked by a colleague whether she should put DOA on the CN. I said no just put 'expired.' "

MIL looks slightly peeved that FIL has high-jacked her time to talk. I remind him we are trying to get MIL's reminiscences down on paper and prompt her to continue before she loses her flow of memories:

'We've had a great life, despite the hardships when we were younger. We are fortunate to be very comfortable in our retirement. We've enjoyed some travelling, when we first retired.We took a trip to America, travelling by coach to various places in Phoenix, Arizona and California. Also a trip to Florida. Hong Kong was an interesting experience. Our friend Pam's daughter lived there, so we met up with her and she showed us around. We also enjoyed a Rhine cruise and coach tours in the UK. Up until we were in our mid 80's we were going with J&K Coaches a local company who really looked after us. We did quite a few 'turkey & tinsel' trips to Bournemouth. When there we took the opportunity to meet up with friend Joan who lived not far away in Christchurch. I palled up with Joan in North London. She also worked at Wellcome but she didn't work in the same department. We used to have lunch together, in the subsidized canteen; you could always get a good meal. I am still friends with Joan. She had her 93rd birthday in 2018 as she's a few months older than me. She lives in Christchurch with her son Ernest, who is Ralph's age but never left home! Those lunches in the canteen obviously had their influence. I still love fish & chips on a Friday. It was certainly handy at the time, because mum didn't have to bother in the evening. It certainly saved on the food bills during quite a difficult time.

I've been very lucky. I've had a great husband, a wonderful family and some extremely good friends. Yes, I've had a very good life indeed.'

There are still more stories to liberate from the Boorman personal archives but that will have to wait for another day.

FOOTNOTE:

Ron actually kept a diary during the war, so one of my next projects is to copy it and have it published. We think the original might be of interest to the Imperial War Museum.

The other thing to mention is that Ron looked after Olive for the best part of ten years after her diagnosis of dementia. He was 87 years old when we recognised similar symptoms in him. We built an annexe to accommodate them both. They would both need considerable support with their failing memories. Sadly Ron died a year after moving in to the annexe, in December 2014. Olive, however, is still relatively robust, despite her memory issues. She tells us she will live to be one hundred.

I can well believe her!

MIL enjoying herself at the resdidential care home.

THE JOY OF DEMENTIA?

Summer 2014

One sunny Tuesday morning I arrive to help my ILs out with any household tasks. I am making cups of tea, when FIL sidles up to me in the kitchen looking most forlorn.

'What's the matter?' I ask, concerned by the look on his face.

FIL opens his mouth and points to a noticeable gap.

He had lost his front tooth. Presumably he had swallowed it. However, as it had a sizeable plate attached to it we are baffled. I was rather sceptical. Surely it was too big to swallow. It would have made him choke. But no, FIL was most convinced he had swallowed it whilst having an afternoon nap, snoozing in the armchair.

'Well, that one will probably come back and bite you in the bum!'

We both chuckled.

For the next week, both Ralph and I were enquiring about the tooth until one Tuesday morning FIL rang, which was quite unusual. I asked if all was ok, as I was due to be there later that day to take them both to the dentist:

'No it's the tooth' he complained.

'So what's happening with the tooth?' I enquire.

'Well, that's the problem....nothing. I just have a very uncomfortable feeling. Perhaps I should mention it to the dentist when we go later.'

'I really don't think the dentist will be interested in a tooth in any other orifice than your mouth.' I retorted, rather briskly, but trying to suppress the giggles. 'We really need to do something about it. This has gone on too long!'

After advice from his GP, I took him to A & E at Queen Mary's, Sidcup. After the long wait for the radiologist for an X-ray, she called me in and said she thought it would not be advisable to do an X-Ray unnecessarily. She didn't think the tooth could possibly be "hiding" in his digestive system. She then referred us to a very sympathetic doctor who also agreed with her.

Our two hours or more at the hospital were a complete waste of time, especially as FIL was unconvinced by their reassurances.

Two weeks later I had an excited call from FIL:

'Guess what. I've found the tooth.'

It had indeed been hiding. Under his bed!

Ron and Ralph looking very smart for Andrew & Marie's wedding. Before Ron's tooth and memory problems.

CHRISTMAS 2014

Greg and Amelia were with us Christmas Eve and Christmas Day as well as MIL and FIL. I was worried it would be a bit dull for them as they normally spend Christmas Day with their cousins of similar age. I did ask brother-in-law Chris,together with nephew and nieces, Andrew, Lucy and Holly but they wanted to have lunch at home. Maybe it was easier for him and the rest of the immediate family rather than have an overwhelming hoard. It was the first Christmas without my sister, Gillian. I think in some ways it was easier on me too as he knew it would be difficult to bring MIL & FIL up to them. I haven't really been to their house too much. Probably avoiding it now my sister isn't there. It seems so empty without her.

I think Greg & Amelia were rather disappointed. However, Greg loves playing games and so when it was suggested we play "What am I" he was very enthusiastic. Amelia was keen anyway as she sees it all as "good therapy".

It was hilarious and probably one of the funniest Christmases ever. The enduring memory of the day will be FIL with a sticker on his forehead that stated: "I am a Pizza". Even with clues he was struggling, so we said it's something you eat fairly regularly and begins with P.

His answer was "Phoenix".

THE JOY OF BAFTAS

14 May 2000

It was not our normal sort of Sunday.

Far from it.

As we were skipping up the Park Lane entrance steps to the Grosvenor House Hotel, the doorman in his exceptionally smart livery, took one look at us and commented:

'I think you are at the wrong entrance. Don't you want to walk the red carpet?'

Despite the humidity plastering our evening attire to our bodies, I guess we did look relatively glamourous. I was tottering along in impossibly strappy, high, diamante heels, my glittering black dress clinging unfashionably to all my unwanted curves. I was rather pleased too with my lilac satin Primani jacket. It's amazing what glitzy look you can achieve for under twenty pounds. Ralph did a fair impersonation of James Bond, shaken but not stirred in his suave and debonair DJ. Despite the discomfort of the additional walk, we headed round to the more impressive front entrance.

There, seemingly awaiting our arrival, were the Nikon and Canon wielding paparazzi. The uninvited were kept from the crimson walk of fame by pristine white ropes looped between slim chrome pillars glinting in the early evening sun.

'Over here!' voices ripped through the still air, hands flapping like demented pigeons trying to attract our attention. Ralph and I first giggling, then willingly obliging. Flinging a cursory wave back. But once they snapped the shot, childish disappointment clouded their expressions. It was a very strange sensation walking along that hallowed carpet, being scrutinised and photographed, just in case you were someone vaguely famous!

We headed into the lobby and were directed to the pre-award ceremony drinks.

We soon found our impossibly glamorous friend, Pascale, already mingling with the other guests. She had invited us to this once in a lifetime 'do' – the 2000 television BAFTA awards - as guests of United Airlines. She was no stranger to these type of events, having been both to BAFTAs and OSCARS before. She was well used to maximising the opportunity of mixing with the "stars". Shameless in fact! When she discovered I had my camera in my beaded black evening bag, she wasted no time whisking it out of my hands. Her mission that evening was to have her guests (and herself) photographed with as many celebrities as possible. We weaved in and out of the crowded room, breathing in wafts of expensive perfume and aftershave mingling with the slightly acrid body odours and alcohol fumes. Trailing Pascale, drinks in hand, we struck up conversations with anyone prepared to chat or just pose for a photo. Within twenty minutes of arrival I had chatted to Sir David Puttnam, trying to create the impression that I was some film aficionado. This was followed by brief encounters with an eclectic mix of personalities: Sir David Frost, Stephanie Powers, Ali G, Lennox Lewis, Ant & Dec, Graham Norton to name but a few well-known names from the guest list.

I also had a brief conversation and photo with the very gracious and charming Joanna Lumley. I couldn't help thinking, though that the obvious plastic surgery had not done her justice. The skeletal appearance of her skin stretched over her skull gave her a rictus looking smile.

It was very surreal but immensely entertaining and the evening had only just begun.

'Will guests please take their seats in the ballroom?' An announcement barked over the Tannoy.

Everyone scuttled towards their seats at the long linen-clad tables. Ours, disappointingly seemed rather far away from the proceedings: we were on the balcony overlooking the stage, with all the celebrities seated on tables below us. Still, we couldn't complain plenty of food and drink arrived, which gave it a cabaret feel. Copious amounts of alcohol flowed that evening; wine and champagne coolers seemed to be the central feature of every table. It's surprising I can actually remember the evening.

Once the award ceremony began we realised we were in fact in a very good position after all. The celebrities collecting their awards had to w alk across the balcony past our table. More photo opportunities. A very drunk Caroline Aherne (of Mrs Merton and Royle family fame), clung onto my arm as if I was her new best friend and then promptly slopped her champagne

over my dress. Not to be outdone, her TV dad Ricky Tomlinson took the opportunity to give me a very sloppy and scratchy whopper of a kiss. My face has never been quite the same since that encounter.

After what seemed an endless procession of celebrities and inevitable photos, the formal part of the evening came to an end. We were invited to join the "after party" which was in another set of rooms in the hotel. But as I looked over the balcony, I caught a glimpse of a very familiar face sitting all alone at his table, seemingly abandoned. Not missing the opportunity, I raced from the balcony, down the winding stairs to the ground floor of the ballroom.

There was my hero, Sir David Attenborough, looking somewhat lost and then a trifle bemused when I asked if I could have my photo taken with him:

'What me?' he questioned, in a completely self-effacing manner.

'Yes please' I nodded enthusiastically and accosted a waiter to take the shot.

'I'm a huge fan of your documentaries, and I must say not a little envious of all your animal encounters. Particularly with those gorillas!'

I wanted to prolong the exchange as long as possible and I asked where all the other occupants of the table had disappeared.

'Oh to have their pictures taken as Radio Times covers'

'That sounds fun' I replied

'Oh I think I'm getting a bit old for all that stuff.'

'You're not old!' I reprimanded, then added:

'Why don't you come and join in?'

'No don't worry about me dear. I'm going off home now. It's been a long night.'

I reluctantly left my all-time hero (apart from Ralph!) to head home to his cocoa and bed.

So it was off to find my replacement real hero (Ralph) and head to the 'games' room. Not only were they taking pictures, but there were casino type tables set up.

Ralph was already in the line for his "cover" picture, as the Liam Neeson character in Star Wars. I took my place at the back of the queue, standing behind a very petite blonde.

It was Barbara Windsor. She was in fact one of the featured Radio Times covers. I couldn't resist commenting:

'This is a bit like carrying coals to Newcastle, isn't it?' she let out her trade-mark giggle and said:

'Isn't it just?'

'So are you going to pose as yourself?' I asked.

'Oh no...I want to pose in that luvverly shell.'

She was alluding to the cover where Charlie Dimmock had posed as Botticelli's 'Birth of Venus'.

'I was thinking as posing as you' I joked.

'Oh no...do the shell' She urged. I took her advice and posed as Venus'.

Photos completed, the guests were shepherded into another room for the after party and we boogied the night away, with our new illustrious friends. Babs jiggling and jiving, the barefoot Charlie Dimmock in her voluptuous red dress, Honor Blackman, Sue Johnson (yes, the Royle family were well presented), various individuals from the soaps and B-listers. Star struck, we stuck it out until the very end, staggering back to our hotel, the Metropole on Edgware Road in the early hours.

Unlike our fellow BAFTA attendees, we were back at our desks at work the following morning, with sore feet and heads, wondering if it had all just been a very glamorous dream.

Pascale chatting with Honor Blackman

THE JOY OF DAWN MUSINGS

JULY 2016

It's 04.00. The barest glimmer of light forcing its way into our darkened bedroom, heralds another busy day, bursting with new challenges and opportunities.

Within just a few minutes my brain, has sprung into action. The neurons, which last night had barely managed a spark, now fizzle and sizzle into unwelcome activity. Ping. It hits the 'What are we doing today?' buzzer. Immediately a vision of a garden pops into my mind. Now with my part-time working I am able to help Christine and Garry in their new house which I haven't seen yet. By Ralph's account it's still not in a very liveable state. They took a sledge hammer to it in March and are now slowly putting it back together. Only last week Ralph got the plumbing up and running. Before we left for their wedding in Jamaica they only had cold running water and no shower. Today I am tasked with sorting out their garden, which is, I am told, a 'bit of a jungle'. I shall be taking my machete, pith helmet, leach bands and thick gloves. No sooner do I start planning my list of other essential items, 'ping' and the gleaming ball of neurons is off, sparks flying, to the opposite corner of my own personal interior pin ball machine. Ping ping ping. 'Mermaids' lights up. Now that's a really high scorer. At least 100 points. The activities from last night flood into my now very active brain. Shame I wasn't as 'on the ball' then! By 7.30pm my brain has definitely lost its' spark and by 9.30pm it is already winding up its' alarm clock and putting out the cat. But I wouldn't miss it. I love the interaction of all those creative minds and the wonderful array of ideas and stories. It is now starting to have a very cosmopolitan feel and the excitement of having another published author is positively tangible. I can't wait to download Sanchia's 'We the Great are Misthought'. Ping Ping Ping. 200 points. The ball is careering wildly to its' next destination: 'Kindle', which is temptingly sitting beside me, like Alice's 'drink me' bottle.

THE JOY OF CREATIVE WRITING

THE DREAM HOUSE

(Short story winner of the 2019 Westgate-on-Sea Literary Festival)

She had never intended to move.

The little Kentish village where she currently resided had been the best place she had ever lived.

Well, apart from Fuegen, in the Ziller Valley, Austria.

Now that was exceptionally beautiful, but it was never a permanent home.

They resided in a small wooden chalet, overshadowed by the looming mountains.

In winter, a sparkling pristine white and in summer a lush vibrant green. She loved watching the beautiful iconic Austrian cows, chewing the cud, with an occasional swish of their tails or quizzically studying her with their doleful brown eyes. The sound of their tinkling bells echoing throughout the valley.

Then the chuff chuff chuff of the jaunty narrow gauge Zillertal steam train, chugging its way slowly along the valley to Mayrhofen. Opening the gingham curtains each morning, the views never failed to amaze and delight her. The only thing missing was Julie Andrews, running down the mountainside singing 'The hills are alive with the sound of music'.

Yet it was merely a ten-month idyll. She had flown out there for a holiday with her new acquired fiancé, Simon. She had never gone back. Simon, a German graduate, helped to manage the other chalets on the sprawling Zillerbad site. An extended holiday after three years at Kent University.

They were both deferring the dreaded moment of entry into the real world. Proper work. Stuffy commuter trains, equally stuffy London offices and the humdrum monotony of work life until retirement. Who wouldn't want to have this brief window of opportunity?

It was a fantastic routine.

They worked in the morning, from February until April, then off skiing every afternoon.

The sense of freedom when you pushed off at the top of the black run, hurtling down the snowy slopes, the icy wind and biting ice crystals bringing a red glow to the cheeks. The adrenalin rush knowing you were seconds from potential disaster. Just a slip, a cross of the skis could send you cannoning down, arse over tit, to potential oblivion. She loved that sensation. She became an adrenalin junkie over those three months.

The summer was tame in comparison.

Until, of course, her sister Melissa and brother-in-law, Alex, came to visit. It was going to be the last big trip in their gleaming, open topped, Triumph Stag. She could not believe her ears when she received the call from her equally surprised Mother:

'Guess what Suzy? You will never believe this….'

'Believe what?' She asked over the crackling static of the landline. Her words travelling thousands of miles along the wires.

'Your sister.'

'What's she done now?'

'Something she said she'd never do.'

She scanned her brain for possible things her sister would not do. There were not that many things. She was the most gung-ho person she knew. She had done it all. She had not only skied, but also dived, hang-glided, paraglided, water-skied, windsurfed, abseiled, rock-climbed and thrown herself out of a plane for charity. The list of her outdoor pursuits were endless. She was struggling to come up with anything. Then it hit her in a brain zinging, tingling flash.

'She's not….'

'Yes she is!' Mum replied.

'I don't believe it. She's really pregnant?'

'Yes! Isn't it lovely? A September baby. I'm going to be a granny sooner than I thought.'

Melissa said she would never have kids. She had already told Mum:

'You are going to have to wait for Suzy to have to provide you with grandchildren.'

No way was she going to have a family. Her dogs were her babies. She lavished such love on her Old English sheepdogs.

Now here they were, her sister and brother-in-law, Tom. A blooming Melissa, struggling to get her already expanding belly out of the low sprung car. In the back, the two bulky frames of the fluffy, drooling Molly and Emma, accompanying the happy couple to Austria. It was hot for the dogs, they had been panting under the penetrating UV rays of the Alpine sun. They were like two cramped yeti in the rear seats of the sporty Stag.

Yes, Melissa was going to have a baby.

That was so long ago now. Her engagement to Simon ended acrimoniously shortly after she returned home. The idyll ended in heartache and poignant, tearful memories. Just an inexpensive Ratner diamond ring to show for the fleeting engagement. At least she had her new niece to distract her from the lingering sadness.

The baby, Danielle, was now thirty years old. A lovelier niece you could not wish to have. Suzy had acquired a baby by proxy, spending many happy hours with her niece as she grew from plump cuddly infant to a long-limbed auburn-haired beauty.

Suzy had moved to her lovely Kent village thirty years' ago, to be close to Melissa and the baby. She was a very attentive auntie, providing much needed help at weekends to her all action sister, who could never keep still.

However, something had changed.

Since retiring, she had found her stunningly beautiful village was in fact the most boring place in Kent.

Nothing happened.

Even the library was only open fifty per cent of the time. A huge waste of a public resource as far as Suzy was concerned.

She had exhausted the delights of the numerous glorious walks. There was one solitary coffee morning, occurring in the drab village hall each week. She had run out of conversation with the other women who attended. They did not seem interested in doing anything other than stare into their coffee cups and eat custard creams. She had found it just a little bit depressing. Is this what her retirement consisted of?

She could not drive, which hadn't seemed a problem when she commuted to London each day. Her husband drove up as he had an underground parking space in his Chancery Lane office. The retirement she had hoped for with lovely days out to the coast or country hadn't materialised.

Her husband died of a massive heart attack after a particular strenuous tennis match at their local club. A huge shock. He had seemed so fit. No heart problems or blood pressure issues. They had made an effort to keep fit, rather than to allow the surplus pounds to accumulate.

Now she had to rely on the infrequent bus services. The train was only once an hour too. That really irritated her. The last train from London was at nine pm. She could not even go to the theatre, which she adored.

The children, however, had provided a distraction during the holidays. She was a very convenient childminder for Jemima and Jack, her niece's young children.

Ironically, she would have loved to have kids, but after several failed IVF attempts, she decided to concentrate on her career. She had been a very successful senior manager, travelling the world extensively both on business and for pleasure with her wonderful husband David.

She found it a bit frustrating though, on the child-minding front, as there was only one rather uninviting playground within walking distance. She could not even take them to the library every day.

Then one day her niece, Danielle, had a day off and they went to the seaside. Normally they would head for Broadstairs, which was one of their favourite Kent coast towns. However, it was always very busy on the beach. You had to fight for your square of sand for the kids to build their sandcastles. In the quaint town, the French tourists would jostle for the space on the narrow pavement.

Instead, they headed to Westgate-on-Sea.

'Oh that's funny' she told Danielle on the car journey. 'I've just remembered. Your grandparents looked at buying a property in Westgate when they retired. Nan was all for it but Granddad decided he could not face the hassle of moving. He didn't really like change. As it happened, you'll remember he died only three years later with tumours on the brain. Nan never did move there. Instead, she had decided to move to our village a few months after I had moved. You may not remember. You were quite small at the time.'

They parked, with ease, alongside the sloping green sward of lush lawn.

Suzy surveyed West Bay. The colourful and artistic well-maintained beach huts, the sandy beach stretching far into the distance on the receding tide, and the neat café, which had a smart upper terrace enclosed in glass, gleaming with an aura of newness.

'I can't believe I've never been here before.' Suzy exclaimed as she sat overlooking West Bay, eating her enormous 99 ice cream she had purchased at the West Bay Café. The kids were playing happily on the sand, whilst she and Danielle sat in her newly purchased tropical themed deck chairs. She had been in the water earlier in the day. They could have been the Mediterranean; the water was so warm.

'This really is a fantastic place' she commented, as she looked back at the rather grand properties, which overlooked the beach. 'It reminds me a bit of Tankerton with the similar sweeping lawns, but it's much more quaint. It has history. No parking problems either. It really is a gem. I can't believe that the kiosk only charges £1.00 for tea and coffee. What a friendly couple who own it. In fact everyone's so friendly here, I spoke to quite a few locals on the way to the kiosk.' After a pause, breathing in the fresh seaside air, she added: 'That new Fin Bar restaurant looks lovely too. We'll have to try it out for dinner.'

'It looks a bit posh, Auntie.' Danielle replied.

'Don't worry, my lovely, it's my treat. I'm just so happy you brought me here today. There's such a lovely vibe about the place. I am totally chilled.'

'Yes, me too.' agreed Danielle, rubbing the sun cream into her legs, which were starting to become a worrying lobster pink from the intensity of the sun. 'When the weather's like this, you wouldn't want to go anywhere else, would you?'

'No, you certainly wouldn't.' agreed Suzy. She then added. 'I wonder what the property prices are like here. I would think the same as Whitstable. Most of the houses seem quite grand and the shops we passed seem rather upmarket.'

In Whitstable, the prices had rocketed since the high-speed train and the 'Whitstable Pearl' series of cosy crime books written by Julie Wassmer. She had done for Whitstable what Colin Dexter had done for Oxford with his 'Morse' books.

When Suzy finally returned home, she was salty, tired and happy. The sea air had revived her sagging spirts. The tang of ozone was so therapeutic. A great restorative. She started to do some research about the area on her laptop.

She didn't realise Margate too was steeped in history. The recently redeveloped Royal Sea Bathing Hospital had been a sanctuary for sick people since 1793. Even First World War veterans went to this hospital to recover. It was certainly a very popular place at the turn of the 19th century. The sea air supposedly a cure for scrofula. She had no idea what scrofula was. She had to look it up online:

'Definition. ***Scrofula*** *is a condition in which the bacteria that causes tuberculosis causes symptoms outside the lungs. This usually takes the form of inflamed and irritated lymph nodes in the neck. Doctors also call scrofula "cervical tuberculous lymphadenitis": Cervical refers to the neck.'*

Now she knew. She hadn't heard of anybody contracting scrofula these days, thank goodness. It sounded most unpleasant.

Suzy, by contrast, felt excited, alive and with a new sense of purpose and vigour. Definitely the best in a long time. Certainly since David died.

Perhaps she should investigate the property prices in Westgate?

She had such a shock.

The first property to pop up on Zoopla was 'The Dream House.'

Just from the first photo, she was smitten.

It was beautiful.

Exactly the sort of house both David and Mum would have loved, if she had been able to afford it.

She read the sales blurb:

'Steeped in history this superb detached Georgian maritime residence constructed in 1791 was the first property to be built in Westgate. The Admiralty commissioned it for the coastguard keeping watch across the Thames Estuary and the North Sea in the years leading up to the Napoleonic Wars. Prior to that Westgate was primarily farmland but by the 1860s it had been developed and become a 'go to' resort for wealthy Londoners looking for a place by the coast and nicknamed 'Mayfair by the Sea'. This property nestles in delightful grounds on the corner of Old Boundary road leading down to the Blue Flag St Mildred's Bay, named after Mildrith, Thanet's patron saint. The house is only a 30-second walk from the promenade and beach but is totally secluded and hidden from view by walls and high hedges. Therefore, it is not really, until you have walked through the gate and down the path to the front door that you really begin to get a feel for this historic building.

Although the property has been renovated from top to bottom, it retains a number of period features such as cast iron fireplaces with the original Admiralty fouled anchor crest motif, high and coved ceilings, panelled doors and ceiling roses as well as the beautiful Georgian staircase. However, because the property is not Listed, modern adaptations have been allowed, such as top quality double glazed sash windows to provide the same appearance as the originals but much better when it comes to noise reduction and insulation. There is an elegant dining room for occasions that are more formal and a charming lounge with a lovely fireplace as well as a study that overlooks the courtyard but also has an original range that actually still works. The extremely well fitted galley style kitchen includes attractive units on both sides, a built in oven, microwave and hob as well as a dishwasher and washing machine and the wonderful old original back door to the garden. The large cellar is ideal for storage including your favourite wines as well as additional freezers. Walking up the lovely staircase to the first floor you will find the galleried landing.

What the Owner says:
"This was my father's family house that my parents took over in 1997. However, at the time it had sadly been left in a somewhat parlous state so my mother made it her mission to not only bring the house back to its former glory but also to enhance it to create a stunning home for the 21st century. This included taking the house back to basics and putting in new plumbing, electrics, a new roof, new windows and also looking to replace with, as near the original as possible, anything that had been damaged beyond repair. The restoration took a few years but we eventually moved in during 2004 and it has been a wonderful family home ever since. However we are now starting a new chapter in our lives and hope that another family will be able to enjoy everything that has lovingly been done a create this warm and welcoming home. We are so close to the sandy beach with

its slipway for launching jet skis and boats and have tennis courts literally across the road. It is only a minute or so to the shops and the mainline station for the high-speed train to London. Westgate is a lovely seaside town. The Blue Flag beaches at West Bay and here at St Mildred's are wonderful for walking the dogs in the winter and swimming in the summer. Westgate is also a very friendly community with a village like atmosphere. It has some charming and individual retail outlets including a unique parade of individual canopied shops and cafes as well as an excellent and inexpensive three screen cinema."

The romance of this lovely place, steeped in such history tugged at her heart. She felt spirals of excitement unravelling the knot of anxiety she had been carrying, since coming home and entering her lonely house.

Then her heart missed a beat when she saw the price.

'OMG!' she gasped. She could not believe her eyes. 'I don't believe it. I could afford it. Who would have thought it?'

The next morning as soon as the hand on her ornate clock had crawled past 09.00 exactly, she was on the phone to the estate agents. Her hands were shaking with trepidation.

On answering, she blurted to the agent:

'I've fallen in love with The Dream House. When can I come and view it?'

***House description courtesy of Town & Country Estate Agents, Cantebury.*

POSTSCRIPT

Yes, I did fall in love with The Dream House. I even put an offer on it! Sadly the sale fell through. But if you want to see the house which inspired the story:

https://media.rightmove.co.uk/50k/49350/73350310/49350_16001780_DOC_25_0001.PDF

Warning – if you don't like psychological or dystopian thrillers skip the following stories!

VENOME PLACE

It started out as a normal day in Venome Place. The office was buzzing with activity. In the vast, ultra-modern office, more than 100 people were busy at their desks. Most were wearing headsets allowing them to tap out their clients' travel requests into Galileo, the Global distribution reservation system.

Those not at their desks were moving purposefully about their duties in the open plan area.

Jenny, the Operations Manager, had an emergency.

Clients had been screaming at her down the phone for travel documents they should have received. It seemed there was some technical problem in the administration area, which was delaying some of the document production. The flu epidemic had taken a grip of the office; staff were thin on the ground. Even her Operations Manager, Neil, was ill. He hadn't taken a day off sick for five years...until today. The supervisor of the document production area had been involved in an accident on the way to work. She would not be in either. She hurried towards the Administration area. Partitioning and glass windows shielded it from the main office. Supposedly to stop the clackety thumps of the ticket and itinerary printers distracting the front line troops. The machines were noisy, although perhaps not as loud as the tinny radio blaring pop music in competition.

The door had a dog-eared sign stuck to it:

'PLEASE CLOSE THE DOOR AFTER YOU!'

Amazingly enough, the last person had actually followed the instruction. Jenny gripped the door handle with some force but it wouldn't turn. It had a faulty handle which reminded her she must get Neil to get it fixed....again. As she was exerting downward pressure, she noticed a strange tingling sensation creeping up her arm as a hot flush. How odd, she thought.

The dooor after a struggle, opened. She crossed to where the administrator, Mark, was sitting. It was uncannily quiet; the radio was off and the printers had stopped. Mark had his back to her. He normally swivelled his head in the direction of anyone entering his domain.

'Mark...' she began but broke off when he still did not turn his head. She placed her hand on his shoulder as she looked at his profile. His handsome face was completely motionless.

'Mark, are you ok?' she said shaking him gently. Still no response.

'Mark, Mark' she shook him more vigorously, her voice several octaves higher.

He was in a completely rigid pose, staring at the screen with unseeing grey eyes, like someone in suspended animation.

'What the f**k's the matter with you Mark? WAKE UP!!!' She shouted, now panicking.

Perhaps he was having some sort of epileptic fit. Was he having a Grand Mal? She remembered reading about the symptoms but was never aware that Mark had this condition. She grabbed his wrist feeling for a pulse. She couldn't find one. Quickly pressing her ear to his chest, she could make out a feeble fluttering heartbeat .Perhaps he was having a heart attack? He was only 23 years old but stranger things had happened.

Jenny rushed over to the door but couldn't open it. The handle was completely jammed now and no matter how hard she rattled it, the damn thing simply wouldn't budge. She hammered on the glass partitioning trying to get someone's attention. No one moved. Everyone seemed to be in a similar transfixed state. What the hell was going on? She must be dreaming. She hammered on the glass again. A tingling flush of terror was seeping through her body. Struggling for breath she started to feel light headed. 'Don't panic' she told herself, inhaling slowly to counteract the fear. Racing to the phone Jenny was already dialling 999 before she realised there was no dialling tone. She pressed the 9 for a line again. Still dead. Running over to phone on the other desk, she tried that one. The same...no dialling tone.

Jenny sprinted back to the door again on unsteady legs that felt as though they belonged to someone else. She really wished they did belong to someone else...that she wasn't part of this hideous scenario.

Kicking at the door furiously, she hardly noticed the pain in her toes. She tugged in desperation at the door handle. Again and again. At last it gave in, relinquishing its hold on the door frame, allowing her escape. In the main office, the fluorescent lights flickered ominously as if the power supply might fail at any moment. There was an uncanny absence of human sound; just the gentle whirring of the computers' fans and intermittent clicks from the flickering lighting. Jenny was breathing noisily, the air rasping at her throat.

Casting her eyes around the office, even petite Joanne – normally the life and soul of the office - was motionless. No life in her blue eyes either.

She moved on quickly to Harry shaking him roughly. No response at all. Just his mouth slightly parted as if a word had died on his lips.

All her colleagues were lifeless dummies; a scene strangely reminiscent of a cheap horror film.

Jenny shivered as droplets of cold sweat prickled uncomfortably all over her body. She had to get out and raise the alarm. She sped to the main reception, grabbed her entry card hanging around her neck swiped the pad on the wall. She shoved the door, expecting it to swing open. It remained firmly shut.

She could no longer contain her panic now, kicking and slamming her body into the door. Pain had become an irrelevance.

'Let me out of this damn prison. LET ME OUT. LET ME OUT. HELP. HELP ME...SOMEBODY....ANYBODY.' She shrieked at the top of her voice.

In desperation she went to the award cabinet and picked out the heaviest Trophy. 'Business Travel News - Agent of the Year Award - 1998' seemed a likely candidate. It weighed a ton. She battered the revered trophy against the glass door with all the force she could muster, until there was an explosion of glass, shattering into a million tinkling pieces.

'Thank God' she gasped, blood dripping to the floor where the flying glass had sliced through her skin. 'Safety glass. My arse!!' She muttered furiously to herself as she launched herself at the lift entrance, prodding the lift call button.

'Hurry up you stupid effing lift' She shouted as she hopped impatiently and shook the dripping blood from her fingers. She watched the numbers light up above the lift area as the lift crawled to the fifth floor.

'Thank God' she breathed a sigh of relief as the lift door opened. She pressed the button for the ground floor. No sooner had the doors closed and the lift descended between floors, the lights extinguished abruptly. The lift juddered to a halt.

Jenny was in complete darkness. Not a pinprick of light. The claustrophobic blackness was bearing down on her, tightening and suffocating around her like a giant deadly python.

....

Daily Mail, 20 April 1999, 123 Die in London Office Tragedy

Police are currently investigating the shocking deaths of 123 staff of the global corporate services provider GTQ International in their central London Office, Venome Place. Security guard, Mick Davison, raised the alarm after finding Regional Manager, Jenny Thornton, semi-conscious in the building's lift. It is reported that Mrs Thornton, 35, was delirious when found. She is currently in a critical condition in the Intensive Care Unit at St Thomas' Hospital. The bereaved families are in a state of shock and no one was available to comment. The police are treating the deaths as 'suspicious' but they have been unable to confirm actual cause of death. Sources have suggested that poisoning might be likely.

The survivor's husband, Jonathan Thornton, 38, stated that his wife had been in negotiations with Abbot & White Venture Capital, who own the building.

'My wife's company were the only tenants left in the building. She had been approached about relinquishing their lease early. The building is on the short list for the Mayor of London's residence but Jenny did not feel it was in the company's financial interests to move.

It seems rather coincidental that this tragic incident has happened. I am sure the police will get to the bottom of it. I am just praying that my beautiful wife recovers from whatever is affecting her. It is ironic that staff jokingly called the building "Venom Place." '

2084 – A Cruel New World

(Shortlisted for the 'Get Writing Challenge 2015 Trophy')

She appraised herself in the gleaming mirror-finished wall. A glossy haired, wrinkle-free but haunted face reflected back. Her trim body clad in its faux chamois body hugging Glove Suit could have belonged to a forty year old. How ironic. Being an 'octo' tomorrow was a cruel twist. She felt like a forty year old. In truth, she felt better than she had at forty. Her replacement joints, eyes, hair and skin were better than the real thing. Had she known all this twenty years ago, she would have made a very different decision.

She did not want to spend too long looking at her seemingly ageless lithe self. It just made her current predicament so much more painful. She double rapped her wrist against the mirror wall. It returned to its clear natural 'window state'. The walls of her super loft apartment had these additional features. She chose them as expensive extras. However, she sometimes liked it 'au naturel' at night, allowing the inky darkness to seep into the room. She gazed out of the window at the pinpricks of light zipping along like microbes in the dark veins of the highway many hundreds of feet below her. How much longer would she be able to view this scene?

A vibrating from the Computerised Hidden Implanted Protocol in her wrist reminded her of the important dinner date waiting. He had asked if she would like to be collected direct from her storey but sometimes she liked to do things the old-fashioned way. Striding over to the vast wall displaying a moving underwater sea scene, a flash of aquamarine dive suit caught her eye. It almost looked like a giant sea creature amongst the beautiful array of tropical fish. The vibrant yellow and black shoals of zebra fish, the ethereal angelfish, turquoise and pink parrotfish and then the rather sinister but beautiful dark stingray gliding with ease. This relaxing backdrop she had also chosen as an extra. She could watch the Virtual Reality Video Replay of herself flitting in and out of the colourful coral caves. She loved watching the VRVR of her diving. The sense of weightlessness, the freedom, the beauty of the underwater world. Coral Island was amazing. A man made water paradise just off the coast at Brighton. Hailed as United Europe's number one pleasure destination, would she ever enjoy its delights again?

She double rapped her wrist on the tropical scene and immediately it morphed back to reality: chrome and glass. The Superfast Loft Lift would transport her 527 storeys to the ground below in six seconds. The descent at such speed didn't even allow her to powder her nose. If she had needed it. Her skin was not only flawless, but had a permanent light tanned glow. She stepped from the pressurised cabin, without even a popping ear. However, anxiety prickled her body as she waited for her would be redeemer's vehicle to arrive.

Would he really be able to re-programme her CHIP for her to evade the OVEP* that she had foolishly agreed to twenty years ago? She, like many others, had opted for comfort and luxury as a trade-off. Live now pay later. The UE authorities had impressed upon her there would be no reversal. Once OVEP was chosen it was immutable. The CHIP in her wrist could not be removed. It was, in fact, just a carrier for the smaller OVEP CHIP which was then transported to the inner recesses of the brain. It might just have been her imagination playing tricks but since stepping out of the lift, she could swear she could hear the tick-tock of its ominous count down.

*Octogenarian Voluntary Euthanasia Programme.

A Christmas Tale

(A short story for 'In Touch' magazine 2017)

It's freezing as I creep out of the house as quietly as possible.

I hope I haven't woken the rest of my family with my early morning regime. It's become somewhat of an obsession. They think I'm mad. Climbing into my sparkling frost-encrusted car, I begin to think so too.

Joining the snaking buzz of dawn traffic, in minutes I'm in the car park adjacent to the river Medway. It's already cluttered with cars. No doubt at 6am the other fanatics have queued beneath the hallowed green portal, awaiting its vast doors to be unlocked. Eager devotees scurrying to worship at their mechanical altars. Their new god: the body beautiful.

In contrast, I hobble through the reception area. The obligatory twinkling Christmas tree seemingly nods at me, surrounded by alluring, sparkly wrapped (but empty) gift boxes.

No muscle-pumping machines for me! The pool beckons. Within minutes, I am slipping into its heavenly embrace. Goggles in place, I dive beneath the deliciously warm water for my daily baptism.

Swimming as far as possible on one breath of air, pearl-like bubbles escape from my lips. Beneath me, the glittering blue mosaic tiles resemble a stained-glass window. It's beautiful and this feels akin to a spiritual experience.

On my first length of the pool, I spot something glinting silver, caught in the filter grille beneath me. I gulp a lungful of air, diving down to investigate. It seems to be a small Christmas tree decoration. I pull, but it won't release. After many ineffectual tugs, I can't hold my breath any longer, I lunge to the surface, gasping like an overweight, oxygen-hungry porpoise. Unabashed, I suck another lungful of air and dive again.

I tug urgently at the silvery thread. This time, the grille comes away. A mass of grey swirling murky water snatches me in a vortex of fury, sucking me towards a black hole. I am thrashing and twisting in the grasp of a malign, surging force, spinning like a demonic top. My eyes bulge, lungs screaming in a silent prayer but I can't resist the force of this bottomless abyss.

The darkness engulfing me starts to clear. I can see a green-tinged light flickering above me. My breathing is laboured but at least I'm breathing. The previous pressure in my lungs disperses through my ears in a myriad of tiny gyrating bead-like bubbles. I have a strange tingling in my legs, which increases to the intensity of a thousand stabbing knives. I look down at my once lily-white flabby legs. They have fused, now bonded into a peculiar shape: an iridescent, green scaly tail. One swish of my new powerful appendage, I burst to the surface. I'm in the cool waters of the river. On the bank opposite, the health club, emblazoned with Christmas fairy lights, winks at me benignly.

I have heard of the fabled Medway Mermaids. I never believed I would unwittingly join their ranks.

Yet there's just one vital question on my mind:

'Do mermaids have a Bluewater? I hope so. I haven't finished my Christmas shopping yet.'

A SELECTION OF SILLY POEMS

Our Secret Garden

Our super-secret garden is joyous to behold
A multitude of flowers, so colourful and bold.
Lavender in abundance, a lure to busy bee,
The purple flowered buddleia fills butterflies with glee.
But my once glorious hostas are sadly another tale,
As the slugs' greedy munching compete with voracious snail.

It started as a project, to clear away the weeds,
Replace with something special, all sprinkled through with seeds;
A pool was one suggestion, for kids to splash and play;
We had to dig forever, forever and a day.

But eventually we had a hole, it really was so big,
The kids were quite delighted and broke into a jig.
They couldn't wait for too long, they wanted to get wet,
They splashed about in great delight before the concrete set.

We've had some lovely evenings, in the twilight's amber glow,
Breathing in the heady fumes of grass fresh from a mow.
We sit and watch the flitting bats catching bugs whilst on the wing.
It fills us with such joyfulness which makes our glad hearts sing.
The thought of bulldozers' wrecking jaws, filled me with such despair,
No more beautiful plants and lawn but houses instead there.

So now I am elated - plans just didn't come to pass
And I still have our secret garden with its flowers and its grass.
We can pass our years of dotage observing birds and bees,
Or keep it looking lovely by digging on hands and knees,
But whatever the weather and season, it will always be there,
Our glorious, secret garden – so beautiful and fair.

FIREFLY

Night, dark and heavy
Wraps around us
Like a soft, sodden blanket.

Night, a tropical cacophony;
Cicadas click and buzz,
Monkeys whoop goodnight blessings.

Night, a delicious symphony;
Geckos add their verbal signature,
Gek, Gek, Gek, Gek Gek - Ohhhhh.

Night and the sea,
Adds its crashing tympani:
Boom, boom, whoosh.

Night, pierced with stellar filigree;
A myriad of shooting stars,
Pirouette and gyrate.

Twinkle, twinkle firefly,
Brilliant in the dark night sky.

Olive's Refrain

I love my bed, I really do,
I could sleep the whole day through.
You can hear my happy snore,
Right outside my bedroom door.

I love my bed, so warm and snug,
Embracing in its loving hug,
But disturb my nap, you'll hear me roar,
'Please go away! Five minutes' more!'

Ode to Ferringhi (Penang) on a Monday
PART 1

Typical British, brolly in hand
We love to explore a foreign land,
Bus 101 from Penang City
To find ourselves somewhere quite pretty.
In Straits Quay, new skyscrapers soar
We disembark at Tesco's store,
Across a four lane busy route,
Dodging traffic, the occasional toot.
We make it to the modern quay,
A stop for coffee and a tea.

We could be anywhere in the world,
Cityscapes, like flags unfurled.
Back on the 101, another ride,
The snaking route, with sea beside
Very scenic, we both agree,
These pleasant views upon the sea.
Then more buildings loom into view:
Concrete towers in varying hue,
McDonalds, Starbucks and KFC,
Is this really the place for me?

PART 2

But past the hawkers, soon you'll reach,
The golden paradise of beach.
Boats bobbing on the azure sea,
With plenty of space for you and me.
But this is Ferringhi on a Monday,
Not sure about it on a Sunday?

Then Thai hikers, clad all in Lycra,
Are drawn to us, like drunks to a bar,
Set themselves up on striped deckchairs,
Their booming music attracts our glares.
But this is Ferringhi on a Monday
Definitely not recommended on a Sunday!

Still Ralph comes back with welcome beers,
We clink brown bottles. Tigers! Cheers!
A few more beers, then we'll be singing,
Along to the sounds they insist on bringing.
But this is Ferringhi on a Monday
Go home Thais and come back Sunday!

Let's not let them spread their influence,

With their hi tech gear, conspicuous affluence

We'll sit here in our knotted hankies,

The original, unsophisticated British Gumbies.

So this is Ferringhi on a Monday,

I'd hate to be here on a Sunday.

Then they air their effing stunt kite.

I start to snarl, my lips I bite.

Kite rips through air, then plunges down.

I'm almost hit. I glare. I frown.

So this is Ferringhi on a Monday

Probably more dangerous than a Sunday.

We've had enough of our neighbours' kit,

We both agree it's time to split,

Back to the bustle of Penang City,

Blistering heat and streets so gritty,

We've not been to Ferringhi on a Sunday,

Not sure it's better on a Monday!

February 2018

An Ode to the Durian

A durian is a curious thing-
Spiny round and green,
You'll spot them piled here and there,
But on a bus they're never seen.

What is this odd comestible?
A creature or a plant?
It smells quite rank and evil,
So don't give it to your aunt!

Yet here in sunny Malaysia
They're equally loved and hated,
You'll find them in every jar
Until you're durian sated!

This smelly fruit's a social pariah,
Of the loftiest degree,
It warns you that it's coming
Then from its stench you'll flee.

So woe betide the passenger,
Who takes them on the bus,
The authorities with fine you
As it causes lots of fuss.

February 2018

The Lizard Lady of Lobos

November 2018

She lives amongst the rocks and sand,
In this hostile barren land.
The seals have fled some years ago,
This Islet made by lava flow.
She swirls around in leopard prints,
Sharing with tourists tips and hints
And pointing out her numerous pals:
The lizards living in the vales
Of volcanic rock, or beneath the plants
That in the wind gyrate and dance.
She feeds the lizards crumbs of bread,
Ensuring they are all well fed.
The lizards love her, everyone
Basking in the fierce hot sun.

THE JOY

OF

LIMERICKS

Sophie's Whale Limerick

There was a wise whale named Wally,

Who could be incredibly jolly,

He lived in the sea,

Which filled him with glee,

And he found a girlfriend called Molly.

by Sophie, aged 7

There was a young girl called Sophie
Whose diet was completely wheat-free
A rich chocolate cake
Would make her tum ache
Sending pains shooting down to her knee

There was a young boy called James,
Who loved playing all sorts of games,
But he'd get in a spin,
If he didn't win,
Calling the victor some very rude names!

There was a sweet granny called Ollie.
Who sometimes could be very jolly;
But on days could be bad
Driving everyone mad,
Poking bums with sharp sprigs of old holly!

There was a cute baby called El,
Who created a horrible smell;
The stench in your nose
Was not one of a rose,
But could have been created in hell!

There was a fine vicar called Hugh,
At church had a bit of a "to do";
A drunk tottered in,

Reeking of gin
Then promptly collapsed in a pew!

There was a tall teenager called Dan,
Who played "Pokémon Go" in a van;
Pikachu at the start
Took him to the White Hart,
Then from there the game went down the pan.

There was a young teacher called Greg,
Who discovered a dinosaur egg;
He took it to school,
Breaking every class rule,
Where it hatched out and bit off his leg!

There was a young lady called Meels,
Who had a fixation with seals;
jumped in the water,
Much deeper than she oughta
Communing instead with the eels.

The Joys of the Elf Walk

6th December 2016

Today it's cold and misty but Nanny and Grandad said we are going on an elf walk.

It sounds exciting.

We walk along the road to Cuxton library. There are a lot of people waiting outside, in their walking boots.

Some have dogs. A relative, Chris, is there with my favourite, Suki. She's friendly, white and fluffy. She sometimes stays at Nanny and Grandad's house and I am allowed to take her for a walk.

Once all the elf walkers have arrived, we set off up the hill, passing houses with Christmas decorations in their gardens. There is even a Father Christmas, fast asleep on someone's lawn. But no elves.

'Why is Father Christmas asleep Nanny? It's daytime!' I ask.

'That's because he has been supervising the elves in the workshops making all the toys in time for Christmas' she replies.

We climb up a steeper hill, then under a railway tunnel. Quite a few of the group (including me) scream and shout in the tunnel. It echoes and is very noisy!

We then walk across a very muddy field. It's hard for me, even in my tiger wellington boots.

'It's very squelchy and slippery' I moan 'My boots are so heavy now I can hardly lift my feet'

'Well walk on the grass then' Grandad suggests 'The grass should take the mud off the bottom of your boots.'

It's hard walking on this field. Most of the grown ups are a long way away. Only Nanny, Grandad and I trail behind.

'Why are they so far away?' I ask.

'Because their legs are more than twice as long as yours.' Nanny says.

I keep walking. Looking out for elves. I think they are all hiding in the woods.

'My legs are worn out' I moan 'Can you carry me Grandad?'

'You're a bit too heavy now James' Grandad says. "....and your boots are very muddy. Perhaps we'll have to do the short cut.'

So Nanny runs ahead to tell the elf walkers that we are going the quicker way back.

It doesn't seem very quick to me.There's another steep, slippery hill so Grandad helped me up. We get to the top, puffing and panting.

'Are we nearly there yet?' I keep asking.

'Not much further now' say Nanny and Grandad together.

But it's quite far. Through a wood, down another hill, over a bridge, then down Tar Tank Lane. Grandad has to carry me part of the way, even with my heavy, muddy boots. He complains:

'James, you are as heavy as a big sack of potatoes!'

'Let's hope we are back at the library before the other walkers, James. You might get a biscuit.' Says Nanny, puffing like Thomas the Tank Engine.

We arrive at the library before the other walkers. I take off my muddy boots and leave them at the door.

It's good to sit on the reading mat after that very long walk. I'm rewarded with a biscuit and a drink. Then I settle down to look at one of my favourite books: 'We're Going on a Bear Hunt', whilst the grown ups chat and drink tea.

I didn't see any elves, but liked the elf walk anyway.

For more information on the Medway Health Walks please see:

https://www.medway.gov.uk/info/200221/a_better_medway/449/health_walks

THE JOY OF GENETIC INHERITANCE

WRITING BY MY KIDS.....

GREG NORTHWOOD - BIOGRAPHY

Nothing to see here! Apart from this poem.....

Alchemy

I stole that silver and made it platinum.

I fathomed a pattern of atoms, smashing

And crashing until it matters,

My rain pitter patters but I stay high and dry.

Skyscrapers are paving over the sunlight,

It's a dark age, an arced phase of the last days

of the last ray, pain pours upon us until the cask'

quakes, our heart aches but we have to let this

moment go, it's the opposite of catch a cold.

If only we could catapult into a future utopia that's

compatible, panic solved it's all over,

But in actuality it's no sofa, maybe I'll take

Some surplus sulphur and turn into the silver surfer

and seal my purpose, learn to sow seeds

to summon serpents.

AMELIA NORTHWOOD - BIOGRAPHY

Amelia also struggled with her reading and writing. More so than Greg. At eight years old she had classified herself "stupid", so at vast expense, she had an Educational Psychologist assessment to prove otherwise.

Dyslexia has always made academic work a struggle for Amelia but she is very determined.

She had a gap year before studying Speech & Language Therapy at Reading University. During that time she spent almost three months in India, teaching English & Maths as part of a government volunteering project (Platform2). She says it was the most "inspirational and life changing period of her life".

Like her mum, she has the travel bug spending time travelling in Thailand, Laos, Vietnam, Australia and Costa Rica.

She now works as a Speech & Language Therapist for Virgin Care in a Kent community hospital.

She has a travel blog but only gets time to write it sporadically as her job eats up her leisure time.

She hopes one day to work in Australia and spend more time travelling (and writing).

BLOG ADDRESS: https://imonmywaytrav3l.wordpress.com

Slummin it (India)

MAY 30, 2018 I'M ON MY WAY TRAVEL BLOG

"India happens to be a rich country inhabited by very poor people"- Manmohan Singh

We enter the "Kathputhli" slum of Jaipur.

A crowd of children skip towards us from their tiny silver lined huts. Kaise ho? "The young Hindi boy enquired. "Main theek hoon." I reply back cheerily. He flashes his surprisingly white teeth in a beaming wide smile at me. I glance down; his feet are smothered in germ infested grime from the crusty ground. His face looks unwashed and he wears torn tatty shorts, with no t-shirt to protect his stick thin withering body. We try to have a conversation, but it doesn't get very far. He carries on speaking to me in Hindi, accompanied by his charming schoolboy smile.
Despite being surrounded by dirt, squalor and flies. He seems happy.

The swarm of children engulf the rest of my group; 42 fresh faced British volunteers. The kids want sweets and are intrigued by the inquisitive foreigners. None of our group has the required sweets but we bring out our phones and they all jump into pictures with us. "Picture, picture picture" they all enthusiastically shout. They giggle, hugging each other, wrapping their arms around the volunteers – their new best mates.
I then turn my head slowly to take in my slum surroundings. In the distance I watch mothers carrying their babies, flashing us bemused smiles. I see towers of loose rubbish and debris. It lurches over their sweltering corrugated iron huts. It's a citadel of shit and rusty materials.

Suddenly we are instructed to leave by our Indian tour guides. We are herded up and then make an abrupt exit. We leave the slums and walk through another run down village. A damp dark tunnelled alley lies ahead of us. We reluctantly walk through it. Mud and animal faeces is splattered all over the ground. I look down and see a small lost baby crying. She is trying to crawl through the sludge. No mother is around to look after her. I want to pick the baby up but our guide angrily tells me not to get involved. We are hustled along and told to carry on walking.

We look at each other in dismay. Where is her mother? Did that really just happen?

No laws on health and safety apply here.

We carry onwards to the next village and the locals greet us. I spot ladies affront carrying pots and wearing colourful sequined saris, flashes of gold, pink and red covering their dark brown bodies. We walk around a bend and enter a small hut covered in mud and dry cow faeces. The hut is pretty sturdy! The shop owner is sitting on the floor sewing beads onto a range of garments. She points to a pile of clothes and shows us a selection of coloured saris and salwar kameez suits to try on. We buy a few outfits from the lady and then get into our minibus.

I say goodbye in my head to the slum dwelling children and the villagers in this poverty stricken area. You'll never be forgotten.

Despite the shitty circumstances, they are incredibly friendly and possibly even happy.

Maybe ignorance is bliss after all?

Some pictures from my India adventures

THE

VERY

FINAL WORD...

FOR MY SURROGATE SISTER, LIZ

In Liz's Shoes

I always longed
To be in Liz's shoes.
The Imelda Marcos of Chatham; wardrobe
Bulging with well-shod shelves, for every
occasion
in dazzling
hue: a shoe.
Glitzy
salsa sling backs.
Soft suede mules. Dolly
shoes, pink, blues, spotted, bowed,
killer heeled,
narrow-
toed,

But now I despair
And don't care
To be in Liz's
shoes. Her
wardrobe is
bare, except for one
pair of Sensible flat
lace ups for support
and her balance, When
what she really needs
is a magical pair of
crystal slippers

Background to this poem

I wrote this shortly after my dear friend (and surrogate sister) Liz, gave me two black bin liners of her shoes.

She was diagnosed with motor neurone disease in August 2017. By February 2018, she could no longer wear her shoes with heels.

Over the subsequent years her mobility and speech deteriorated.

Despite that, she remained independent, determined and inspirational. She went to to Westminster speaking on behalf of those with MND to the All Party Parliamentary Group. She continued to work as Kent Community Foundation's Office Manager until she could no longer speak.

She was, for most of her life, involved with the charity sector, working in both Scotland and England. She moved home 17 times in her life, following job opportunities.

Liz always helped others.

The inevitable happened in February 2021.

MND won the battle and claimed Liz as another victim.

Please help the Motor Neurone Disease Association to support the research to find that magical crystal slipper – a cure for this awful condition.

Let's try to make a world free from MND.

Every little helps :

https://www.justgiving.com/fundraising/judith-northwood-boorman2

Ingram Content Group UK Ltd.
Milton Keynes UK
UKHW011846190623
423702UK00001B/222

9 781803 026039